# If This Is the Way the World Works

# If This Is the Way the World Works

## Science, Congregations, and Leadership

*William O. Avery*

*Beth Ann Gaede*

THE ALBAN INSTITUTE

Herndon, Virginia
www.alban.org

The Alban Institute
2121 Cooperative Way, Suite 100
Herndon, VA 20171

Library of Congress Cataloging-in-Publication Data

Avery, William O., 1943-
  If this is the way the world works : science, congregations, and leadership / William O. Avery, Beth Ann Gaede.
    p. cm.
  ISBN-13: 978-1-56699-355-5
  1. Leadership—Religious aspects—Christianity. 2. Leadership. 3. Christian leadership. 4. Science—Philosophy. 5. Religion and science. I. Gaede, Beth Ann. II. Title.
  BV4597.53.L43A94 2007
  253—dc22
                          2007035658

    12   11   10   09   08   07       VG      1   2   3   4   5   6

# Contents

v

117082

# Preface

$\mathcal{W}$E HAVE BEEN STUDENTS OF LEADERSHIP LONG ENOUGH TO HAVE seen various understandings of leadership come into and fall out of favor. Bill—the Larson Professor of Stewardship and Parish Ministry and professor of field education at the Lutheran Theological Seminary at Gettysburg, a seminary of the Evangelical Lutheran Church in America (ELCA)—has taught leadership courses for several years and, among other courses, continues to lead a required seminar for seniors on pastoral leadership. Beth, an ELCA pastor, began asking questions about leadership during her years in parish ministry and has continued to explore the topic since she began editing resources for congregation leaders nearly two decades ago. We both have studied checklists of leadership traits, completed assessment tools to determine our preferred leadership style, puzzled over the leadership style required in various challenging situations, and sometimes felt overwhelmed by the plethora of books and other resources available on the topic of leadership.

Leadership studies can be traced back at least to Plato, the first thinker to systematically examine the purpose of the state and the function of the leader. In their helpful book *Reviewing Leadership: A Christian Evaluation of Current Approaches*, scholars Robert Banks and Bernice Ledbetter outline the history of "modern" leadership studies. They point to the field's beginnings in the latter half of the nineteenth century, when the notion that history is the story of "great men" and their impact on society was central to the understanding of leadership.

In the first half of the twentieth century, attention shifted to identifying traits—the personalities, personal talents, skills, or physical character-istics—of these great men. The next phase of study, throughout the 1950s and '60s, focused on leaders' behaviors and styles. In the 1970s and '80s, more attention was paid to the context of leadership, as well as to the fit between various styles and particular contexts. Others fo-cused on the situation and the need for leaders to adapt their approach to fit the circumstances. The distinction between transactional and transformational leadership, which recognizes the importance of the relationship between leaders and followers, became influential in the late 1980s. The field of leadership studies continues to expand. Banks and Ledbetter note that over the past two decades, many thinkers have developed complex theories about how leadership operates and develops, taking into account a wider array of factors, including the place of personal and organizational values and responsibilities and the increasingly multicultural and global nature of organizations.[1]

In our ongoing reading about leadership, we each discovered the work of Margaret Wheatley, who writes and teaches about how we can live together harmoniously. In her award-winning book *Leadership and the New Science: Discovering Order in a Chaotic World*, Wheatley lays out a series of principles from quantum physics and suggests implications of each principle for leadership. She focuses on

> the meta-issues that concern those of us who work in organizations: Where is order to be found? How do complex systems change? How do we create structures that are flexible and adaptive, that enable rather than constrain? How do we simplify things without losing what we value about complexity? How do we resolve personal needs for autonomy and growth with organizational needs for prediction and accountability?[2]

Wheatley argues that "leadership is best thought of as a behavior, not a role," and that leaders are best thought of as people who "emerge from the group, not by self-assertion, but because they make sense, given what the group and individuals need so that they can survive and grow."[3]

When we encountered Wheatley's work, we quickly found our-selves thinking, *Here is a perspective that can help us think in new ways about congregations and how to lead them.* Although we use science differently from Wheatley, as we discuss in our introduction, her work inspired us to ask two questions. First, what principles from science are so broadly accepted that scientists themselves are willing to say, "This is the way the world works"? Second, how do congregations and their leaders behave when they operate in concert with these seem-ingly universal principles? Our premise is that congregation leaders are most effective when they lead in a manner consistent with the way the world—God's world—works.

Although Wheatley's work was the impetus for this book, we both have been influenced by a variety of other thinkers in the leadership field. We especially value the work of Harvard professor Ronald Heif-etz, particularly his book *Leadership Without Easy Answers* (Belknap, 1994). We appreciate his clarity, rigorous definitions of basic terms such as *leadership* and *authority*, focus on the needs of the systems being led, and creative thinking about leading without authority—an especially fertile concept for congregations, where many leaders carry out important work without authority. Like many Christian leaders, we value Quaker Robert Greenleaf's extensive work on servant-leadership, the principle that the leader must first attend to the needs of others and the organization as a whole and must particularly serve the least privileged in society. A foundational book for us has been Peter Senge's *The Fifth Discipline* (Doubleday, 1990), regarded as one of the most important management books of the past twenty-five years. Senge describes a healthy company as a learning organization focusing on human values to instill vision, purpose, and reflection, and using systems thinking. We have also been influenced by the work of Peter Block, including his books *The Empowered Man-ager* (Jossey-Bass, 1987) and *Stewardship: Choosing Service over Self-Interest* (Berrett-Koehler, 1996), in which Block details the advantages of flattening the hierarchical structure of most companies. Finally, the writings of Jim Collins—books such as *Built to Last* (Harper and Row, 1994) and *Good to Great* (HarperCollins, 2001)—offer important tools for examining the characteristics of companies such as Abbott,

Gillette, Kimberly-Clark, Pitney Bowes, Walgreens, and Wells Fargo, companies that have exhibited exceptional leadership and remained model corporations over many decades.

Of course, thinkers outside the realm of leadership studies have influenced our views about congregation leadership too. In particular, trained as we are in the disciplines of Lutheran theology, we almost automatically examine life through theological lenses, interpreting our experience through our theology and fine-tuning our theology to reflect our experience. You will find references to our theological foundations from the introduction through the conclusion, because our insights about pastoral and lay leadership are anchored in our central theological understandings.

Central to Bill's theology is the good news that God accepts us humans not on the basis on our lives but solely on the basis of God's love. We are marked by the sign of the cross in our baptism, indicating God's eternal love for us, and therefore we are *free from* trying to earn God's favor and *free for* serving our neighbors and all of creation. God's loving pursuit of us reached its zenith in the life, death, and resurrection of Jesus, God's Son, our Lord. God continues to be active in this world and in our lives through the Holy Spirit. In other words, this good news comes from a relational triune God. God is Immanuel, "God with us," and "with" is the language of love. God does not take us over as if we were mere puppets, but rather God is lovingly with us, with others, and with God's whole creation. This means that God suffers with humanity and all creation when we suffer and rejoices with us and the world when we rejoice. We Christians also suffer with the suffering of humans and the world and rejoice in their joy. God's invitation to follow God is without strings. It is never "If you serve others worthily enough, then I (God) will continue to love you," but "Because I love you without reservation, therefore I ask you to love and serve others as I do." While Bill finds it impossible to select only one biblical text as central to him—it depends on the context—certainly the familiar words of John 3:16-17 are especially dear to him: "God so loved the world that he gave his only Son, so that everyone who believes in him may not perish but may have eternal life. Indeed God did not send the Son into the world to condemn the world, but in order that the world might be saved through him."

Central to Beth's theology is the image of *Christus Victor*, God's work through the suffering, death, and resurrection of Jesus Christ to conquer the powers of sin and death in the world. One passage in particular gives her a sense of hope and purpose in daily life and as she thinks about the future of the world: "If anyone is in Christ, there is a new creation: everything old has passed away; see, everything has become new! All this is from God, who reconciled us to himself through Christ, and has given us the ministry of reconciliation; that is, in Christ God was reconciling the world to himself, not counting their trespasses against them, and entrusting the message of reconciliation to us" (2 Cor. 5:17-19). God's healing work in the world was not a one-time event; it goes on even today, and we are called to be instruments of that healing.

As we explored Wheatley, we found that although she begins with science, not theology, and does not explicitly address a Christian audience in her work, her ideas are consistent with our own theological assumptions. We especially noted her concern for growth and harmony in individuals and systems, interests we share, given our understanding that individuals and faith communities are called to a unity in Christ that affirms the interrelatedness of all creation and carries God's message of reconciliation to the world. Following Wheatley's contention that principles from science can inform our understanding of systems and leadership, we invite clergy and lay leaders to reflect with us on five principles from science that describe "the way the world works," ideas we find consistent with Scripture and Christian tradition. It is our conviction that when faith communities align themselves with these principles, they more faithfully carry out their vocations as witnesses to God's reconciling work and as servants to one another.

# *Acknowledgments*

THIS BOOK WOULD NOT EXIST WITHOUT THE GENEROUS ASSISTANCE of nearly two dozen working scientists; teachers of theology; and lay leaders and clergy who serve in congregations, seminaries, denominational offices, community organizations, and in retirement. They met with us in groups and individually, talked on the phone with us, and responded at length to our e-mails, working hard to help us draw connections between science, theology, and congregational life and leadership, and to prevent us from distorting scientific principles or ignoring the realities of congregational life. We are grateful for the conversations we enjoyed with Carol Albright, John Albright, Ted Davis, Richard Headen, Mark Vitalis Hoffman, Leonard Hummel, Jeff Imhoff, Kathleeen Kastilahn, Jeff King, Connie Kleingartner, JoBeth Marshall, Terry Nichols, Mary Robinson, Jeff Sartain, Sally Simmel, Bob Sitze, Jean Morris Trumbauer, Jane Vennard, Jan Viktor, Jann Weaver, Cletus Wessels, Margaret Wheatley, Roger Willer, Grace Wolf-Chase, and Gayle Woloschak.

Throughout the book, readers will find occasional quotes from these consultants, although we do not identify each speaker or writer by name. Our decision not to quote these conversation partners by name in no way reflects a lack of respect for their expertise and wisdom. Rather, we want to emphasize not the science itself and "what so and so said," but the insights we gleaned from these examples of scientific thought and thoughts about science, congregations, and leadership. We authors take sole responsibility for our interpretation of the rich conversations we enjoyed.

# Introduction

*A*S READERS OF NUMEROUS BOOKS ON LEADERSHIP, WE AUTHORS have become weary of lists—"Thirty-seven Proven Ways to Be the Best Leader of Your Organization" or "Fifteen Steps to Effective Leadership." On the one hand, we are persuaded that there is no one perfect way to lead, because what constitutes effective leadership varies greatly depending on circumstances, personalities, relationships, goals, beliefs, and purpose. On the other hand, we are convinced that there is a better way to *conceive* of leadership. We believe organizations could fulfill their purposes more faithfully, reach their goals more efficiently, and treat their participants and constituents more respectfully if leaders in business, government, and the not-for-profit world, including the church, changed the way they view leadership. We also believe that by following basic scientific principles, we arrive at a different view of leadership in social organizations such as the church.

The characteristic way a people experience and interpret the world is called their worldview. Worldview refers to the perceptual framework used to understand reality and incorporates one's religious, political, cultural, and scientific beliefs. Principles such as the idea that all adults should be able to choose who will govern them or that certain human rights are universal are elements of particular worldviews. We know language both helps form and limits worldview and that even a slight change in one's worldview generates new insights into reality.

For instance, English speakers tend to think first of "family" as the nuclear family—father, mother, and two kids. The Hebrew and Greek languages, however, have no exact equivalent for family. Instead, these languages use words translated into the English "house"—the house of Abraham, the house of David. Notice that the concept of family in Hebrew is broader, including not only grandparents, aunts and uncles, and cousins, but also, if the family is wealthy enough, slaves and servants. But also notice that the meaning of house is different in the two languages. In English we usually think first of house as a building, a physical structure, but in Hebrew and Greek house first means "household"—encompassing many relationships—and only secondarily does it refer to a physical building. The way we understand "family" and "house" will affect the way we understand our relationships with potentially a great many people.

We also know that worldviews change over time. For example, current understanding of the relationship between the earth, planets, sun, stars in our galaxy, and bodies and forces beyond is very different from the view held for centuries before Galileo—that the earth was the center of the universe. Consequently, many people today no longer see humanity as the center of the universe but view the human community as one member in a vast complex of entities. Some periods, such as the Renaissance (fifteenth and sixteenth centuries) and the Enlightenment (eighteenth century), and perhaps the contemporary postmodern period, bring more rapid changes than other, stabler periods in history. However, worldviews are continually being modified.

Worldview is very important to Judaism and Christianity because of the way we conceive of God. Both religions recognize that, in part because of our inescapable worldview, we are severely limited in our ability to know God, even while other faiths may claim to be able to decipher and "find" God. Our worldview necessarily influences, and sometimes distorts, our perceptions, so we cannot see God—or anything else—perfectly clearly. Further, Christians claim we can know the triune God not directly but only as God chooses to reveal Godself to us. We understand that God revealed Godself especially through the Israelites, and most particularly in the life, death, and resurrection of Jesus Christ, through whom God totally immersed Godself in this world. In these three acts—creating and loving the world; choosing a particular people, Israel, as an example to the world; and becoming actual flesh in Jesus of Nazareth—God forever confirmed the importance of this world. God's affirmation of the world is not confined to the past, however. God continues to create and be present in this world through the Spirit, and as the apostle Paul tells us, through the church, which is called to be an extension of Jesus (the body of Christ). Because the world matters to God, the world matters to all who claim allegiance to the triune God. The situation in life of God's revelation is always important, because God reveals Godself not only through timeless truths, but through actual events and particular people in the world. Jesus, we confess, is God's eternal revelation of God. But how we understand the world—our worldview—influences how we comprehend God's work in the world. Behind any claims we might make that "this is the way the world works" lies a deep and pervasive worldview that can shape and inform our understanding of systems and leadership. Listen to the way Carol Rausch Albright, who writes in the area of neuroscience and theology, puts it in her book *Growing in the Image of God*:

> Our thoughts about ourselves, and our thoughts about God, in-
> evitably rest within our sense of what our world is like and how it
> works. . . . Many of us believe that certain teachings about spiritual
> matters are eternally true. But even so, we cannot help but view
> these teachings through eyes conditioned by the intellectual and
> social milieu that molds us—by the prevailing understanding of
> "the way things really are."[1]

We are convinced that science provides a basic worldview by which we twenty-first-century people interpret at least the physical aspects of this universe. Scientists tell us that the world is not flat; the sun is not the center of the universe; the universe is billions of years old; and if we compare the 4.5 billion years of the earth's existence to one hour, humans have existed only for the past ninety seconds of the hour.

## *Science and Theology: Promise and Limitations*

We appreciate the advances in knowledge that scientific inquiry has brought and assert that within the basic premises of science lie certain attitudes and approaches that suggest the most effective way to exercise leadership in a community of faith. Three basic premises of science in the macroworld are foundational for this book. First, scientific inquiry assumes that *the world is regular and understandable.* The evidence that this assumption is valid is that science works so well in explaining our world. Second, in the words of a physicist we interviewed, "The assumption of science is that *things can be tested.* In science, you want to make statements, and statements are not scientific unless you can subject them to the possibility of being falsified by some kind of observation . . . or experiment." Third, and critical for our use of science, *some kinds of questions*—questions of value, meaning, and purpose—*cannot be answered by science.* As our physicist put it, "If a statement cannot even in principle be disproved, then it is not science. It still may be a very important statement—a theological statement—but it is not a scientific statement."[2]

We acknowledge, of course, that in the United States, peoples' attitudes toward the veracity and importance of science vary greatly. At one end of the spectrum are those who, in the words of an observational astrophysicist, "treat scientists as the verbalizers of gospel truth." At the other end are those who dismiss all science as opinion. An example of the latter is people who believe in creationism—arguing that the world, from its beginning to the advent of humans, came to be in six days, in accordance with a literal interpretation of Genesis 1. We place ourselves between these extremes as scholars who take seriously both science and religion, and seek to incorporate both into our worldview.

We are very concerned about the seeming anti-intellectual bias shown by religious adherents who, based on their reading of the Bible, oppose scientific concepts such as evolution and the age of the universe. We believe God created us with minds and imagination so that we would use them. Our faith, in the famous dictum by Anselm of Canterbury, is "faith seeking understanding." We want this book, in part, to stand over against those who reject science on religious grounds. We affirm that science and its worldview not only must be taken very seriously, but also contain basic points that may help us see leadership in social organizations, such as congregations, differently.

On the other hand, we also understand that science has limitations that often are not recognized by the general public or even by some scientists themselves. Science is limited to observable, verifiable claims. Within this parameter, science has revolutionized our view of the world and how we live. Think, for example, of the way our understandings of bacteria and viruses have changed the way we know diseases to be transmitted and cured. Or how the invention of the combustion engine has changed how we travel, where we live, and where we get our food from. The computer and the Internet are changing our lives today more rapidly than we can keep up with, given the explosion of information available to us on any conceivable topic. However, science cannot address questions of purpose and meaning, which, we assert, must be addressed by religion.

Further evidence of the limitations of science is that scientific data and experiments are themselves based on theories. They are not strictly about isolated "true facts" but always involve underlying values. As Albright explains, "Today it is generally acknowledged that all kinds of data and experiments are 'theory laden,' and that theories cannot be proven using only the results of observation. Along these lines, philosophers speak about the 'underdetermination' of theories by empirical facts as a real feature of the scientific procedure."[3] In other words, even the theories that will be tested by analyzing data go beyond pure science to questions of value and purpose. Furthermore, the results of scientific inquiry often lead to consequences that reach beyond science itself.

The observational astrophysicist we interviewed, who studies the possibility of life in other parts of the galaxy, provides a good example of the way scientific data connect with and are even dependent upon questions of value. According to her, with today's advances in technology, it may be possible within the next generation to discover whether "life" exists in nearby solar systems. This very quest raises theory-laden questions, such as, what constitutes life? and what would we recognize as life? Certainly, biologists must join with astrophysicists to address these questions, but do these questions not extend beyond science? Does Christianity have anything to say about what constitutes life? Next, if "life" is discovered, what should we do or not do about this life? Do we leave it alone or intervene? This is an ethical question. Such questions demonstrate that scientific insights often point beyond themselves to questions about underlying values. Hence, as theologians we conclude that a religious point of view is critical for society.

We advocate a two-way conversation between scientists and Christians—rejecting the claim by some scientists that science deals with reality and that nonscientific endeavors such as religion do not. As one of our consultants put it, "We, as people of faith, find some constraints about what we can say about human beings and the universe based on what science tells us, but it is a mistake to make this a one-way conversation, as if science can tell us what we can say." Admittedly, the scientific community does have, as one of our interviewees put it, "a fundamentalist element, that is, if it can't be empirically validated, and if it's not science, if it's not easily qualified as science, then it is not important, not relevant, and [those scientists] will not address it." But just as we reject a fundamentalist approach to theology, we reject such an approach to science. As theologian Phil Hefner has stated, "Meaning will not show up in the test tube, so to speak, but we put it in the test tube. There will always be the need for a so-called 'leap of faith,' as the existentialist philosophers put it."[4] Hefner contends that all assertions of meaning require a leap of faith. "Certainly there is an 'objective' world out there, a world that is prior to us, that operates according to laws we did not invent, and that we must adapt to. . . . At the same time, we have no access to this world except through the ideas that we construct. . . . All science bears the marks of such constructivism."[5]

At the opposite end of the spectrum, very few scientists, in the words of our physicist consultant, "use science as a God detector" and arrive at a position called "intelligent design." Along with the vast number of scientists and theologians, we also reject this claim. One cannot "prove" God's existence from science. Nor, in our opinion, can science lead us to faith, because God is *always* hidden in this world. God has acted, is acting, and will act in this world, but God's way is always hidden. That is why we claim Christianity by faith, not by sight.

Among both people of faith and scientists, and people of faith who are scientists, then, are those who believe theology and science have nothing to do with each other and those who merge or at least confuse the two realms. We said above that we value science. But how do we understand the relationship between science and theology? A theology of the cross lies at the center of our theological viewpoint and informs our view of the relationship between science and religion. The theology of the cross states, in part, that God is always active in this world but in the same way God was active on the cross. In other words, God's acting in this world is always hidden under its opposite: weakness, helplessness, and powerlessness. When we look to see God overcoming death on the cross, what we "see" instead is defeat and death. Martin Luther talked about this phenomenon as God's masks. God's power is always hidden in weakness; God's strength is always concealed behind the mask of impotence. By a leap of faith—not because we can prove it—we believe in Christ's resurrection. We believe that what we "see" as powerlessness on the cross is actually a power that overcomes death itself. We believe that this same God continues to be active in our midst, although still remaining hidden from "detection." As the psalmist confessed, "Your way was through the sea, your path, through the mighty waters; yet *your footprints were unseen*" (Ps. 77:19, emphasis added).

Therefore, we affirm a universe that may be understood without the necessity of God. Dietrich Bonhoeffer called such an understanding the "world come of age." We do not need to posit the idea of God to understand how the world works. The world is understandable without God. Science, we affirm, must be an atheistic enterprise. It must proceed without the premise of God— "as if" God did not exist. Of course, we insist on a science that recognizes its limitations. We believe the most important questions are ones science cannot answer. As one scientist put it, "These are the ultimate questions, the value questions, or even the 'why' questions rather than the 'how' questions. Why is there something rather than nothing? What is the point of the universe? These are not scientific questions. One of the purposes of theology is to address questions like these."

## Margaret Wheatley: Promise and Limitation

The inspiration to use science to envision a different way of leadership in congregations came to us initially from reading Margaret

Wheatley's provocative book *Leadership and the New Science*. In this book, Wheatley outlines as "new science" the twentieth-century insights from relativity, quantum mechanics, and chaos theory. Then, applying these scientific insights, she develops a theory of leadership. At this point, scientists, especially physicists, complain that nonscientists such as Wheatley have misunderstood and misapplied quantum theory to organizational leadership.[6] Every scientist we spoke with told us that it is illegitimate to draw direct parallels from quantum mechanics and chaos theory to leadership of institutions. As much as we value Wheatley's work, therefore, we have taken a step back from Wheatley's use of science.

To understand scientists' complaint, we need to examine the scale of quantum events. Scientists agree that quantum physics is important because it explains many features of our world that are otherwise inexplicable. Quantum theory does this by examining the submicroscopic world of very small electrons and photons. An atom is about $10^{-8}$ (one hundred millionth) of a centimeter. If the atom were expanded to the size of the dome of St. Paul's Cathedral in London, the nucleus of the atom would be the size of a pea, and the electrons would be a few specks of dust moving around inside the dome.[7]

Only with the invention and use of high-speed computers have scientists been able to create a virtual world, the quantum world, that by positing the microworld of photons and electrons explains physical reality. Quantum physics remains a theory, but it is offered by scientists because it explains, better than any other theory, how the universe operates. One physicist calls it "one of the most successful and influential scientific theories of all time."[8] British particle physicist and Anglican priest John Polkinghorne elaborates:

> Nevertheless, all of us who work in quantum physics believe in the reality of a quantum world, and the reality of quantum entities like protons and electrons. The basic reason we believe this is not because they are objective in the classical sense—because they are not—but because the supposition of their existence enables us to understand, to a great extent, physical experience. Thus, intelligibility is the guarantee of reality, rather than objectivity.[9]

Expressed another way, quantum theory is essentially mathematical. Polkinghorne is enchanted by this insight, "One of the fascinating things about the physical world is that its fundamental structure seems always to be expressed in beautiful mathematics."[10]

The problem with nonscientists applying quantum theory to, for example, social systems is twofold: (1) nonexperts vastly oversimplify quantum theory, distorting what the theory means; and (2) nonexperts draw an immediate but unwarranted analogy between the microworld and the macroworld, although Newtonian physics applies in the macroworld. Critic John Hastings notes, "Traditional physics is usually referred to as 'classical' physics and this is still the physics that is used for the everyday, macroscopic world."[11] Insights from quantum theory about the microworld largely disappear in the macroworld we experience daily. Take, for example, the uncertainty principle. Quantum physics shows that the behavior of a single electron cannot be predicted, and hence uncertainty seems to replace predictability. However, in the macroworld, the unpredictability of individual electrons "does not matter very much."[12] Rather, in the macroworld, the numbers of electrons and photons involved in events is so large that the uncertainty principle becomes negligible, and probability can be calculated. Therefore, quantum theory cannot be used to imply that the future is totally unpredictable. Yes, there are limits to predictability, but in our everyday world many things can be predicted with great precision.[13]

While we acknowledge the validity of such complaints, we find Wheatley's insights inspiring and suggestive, especially as she challenges much current leadership theory. Describing her vision as a "minority voice," even though the original edition of her book has been out since 1992,[14] she traces an alternative way of looking at the world through "new science" and then suggests a novel way of imagining leadership of organizations, based on a worldview seen through the lenses of the "new science." Her work helped us reframe the whole endeavor of leadership in congregations by enabling us to shift paradigms. So, while we understand the complaints about the way she uses science, we also believe she makes significant contributions to leadership studies. Although our insights about congregation leadership are somewhat different from Wheatley's, we acknowledge the debt we owe her. Indeed, some of our insights about congregation leadership complement what Wheatley has written, even if we refrain from drawing parallels from quantum physics.

Above all else, we want to use science responsibly. We recognize that even when we base our science on universally acknowledged features, still the matter of making a direct transfer to congregation leadership is problematic. For example, we know that evolution is a principle underlying all biology, and that in the emergence of species, "evolution" has a specific meaning and describes how natural selection occurs. But we must not make direct parallels outside the context of biological systems—for example, to the evolution of language or the evolution of communities. Yes, our scientists agreed, evolution can be applied to other arenas, but we need to be deeply cautious when doing so. We will attempt to keep this caution in mind whenever we draw inferences from science.

## *Philosophy of Science and Leadership of Congregations*

Although we will not be following Wheatley's reliance on quantum physics, we have not simply put Wheatley's insights about leadership in the trash heap. Wheatley herself acknowledges that she did not need to rely on quantum mechanics for many of her insights into leadership, insights we often find compelling. In fact, in a more recent book, *Finding Our Way*, she discusses her leadership theory with scarcely a reference to quantum physics.[15] Furthermore, she admits that she used "new science" for a particular purpose in her earlier book: "I realized that I was using the science to get the attention of those who could hear this message in no other form."[16]

While we will not simply apply Wheatley's scientific concepts to congregation leadership, neither will we abandon her approach—drawing on science to explore leadership. Yes, we understand that it is irresponsible to make leaps from the microworld to our macroworld or from quantum mechanics to congregation leadership. However, even as the scientists we consulted rejected using quantum mechanics for such purposes, they also pointed to areas in the philosophy of science that are almost universally recognized and from which they suggested we might, very cautiously, draw some analogies for congregation leadership. We will not use specific scientific theories but basic, broad, widely accepted principles from the philosophy of science and see how these might affect leadership in U.S. congregations in the early part of the twenty-first century. Our principles derive primarily from the philosophy of science rather than science itself—from theories that overlay scientific experiments rather than the experiments themselves.

From our interviews, we identified five areas from the philosophy of science that, in our opinion, suggest an alternative way to view congregation leadership. We will first explore a basic attitude toward scientific inquiry that has promising implications for change in congregations, and then we will examine four principles from the philosophy of science that point to an overhaul of our view of congregation leadership. Even as we lay out this scheme, we understand that any enumeration is only a heuristic tool and that these principles overlap with one another in a world where everything is connected with everything else. That said, these are the principles on which we will build.

### Information: God's New Thing

The scientific enterprise is always open to new information or data. There is a kind of perpetual edginess to science—a willingness to seek change in order to obtain a more accurate or fuller understanding of the physical world. Science expresses the best that we can know for today but continues to test and explore, with the result that what we "know" today may be wrong tomorrow, or in a generation, or in a century. Just as religious people understand that we now "see in a mirror, dimly" (1 Cor. 13:12), so scientists understand that they do not yet have "answers" to many of the questions we ask about creation.[17] Thus, scientific inquiry is a process, as is life in a community of faith. Openness to a different future, an attitude scientists cultivate, will enhance the health of any congregation.

*Complexity: An End to Childish Ways*

A scientific theory that bears fruit for leadership in congregations is *complexity theory*, which is rooted in concepts of *self-organization* and *emergence*. Albright explains, "By *self-organization* we mean observations that natural systems have a tendency to become more intricately organized all by themselves, without human intervention. New and unforeseen phenomena occur as a result; this process is called *emergence.*"[18] That is, cells divide and become molecules, molecules become organisms, and so on. From the processes of emergence, scientists conclude that the whole is greater than the sum of its parts. The whole brings into being new things different from the constituent elements. For example, hydrogen and oxygen are very different elements from their combination, water ($H_2O$).

Moreover, we understand science to tell us, in the words of one scientist, that "systems function best when there are certain things you can depend on and certain things are open for innovation. Systems can be too orderly, which leads to an oppressive atmosphere, and systems can be too disorderly and are not able to function." We authors state this point in contrast to certain organization-system gurus who suggest that self-organization will keep organizations from dissolving into chaos. That is, it has become commonplace to ask communities of all stripes—corporations, civic organizations, congregations—to embrace chaos at all levels in the belief that self-organization will save the organization from destruction. Instead, we have learned that systems' need for a balance between basic order and disorder is fundamental, and we believe this concept is worth further exploration. While we want to be cautious about drawing implications, without qualifiers, from science to social organizations such as congregations, we believe we can learn about congregation leadership from this scientific theory.

*Interrelatedness: Reconciling the World*

Another key scientific insight is the interrelatedness of all that exists. All reality is made of the same material. That is, rocks and humans and stars of distant galaxies all have the same DNA. Over the long haul, everything is connected to everything else. Given the basic unity of all reality, relationships become critical. Developing relationships is as important as formulating a mission statement or setting goals for the next year. Indeed, the best way to attain goals may be to attend to the relationships in the community, because relationships form the bedrock for outreach and evangelism. Congregations need to create an inviting community to which people may invite others. Furthermore, it is crucial for relationships that information be freely and fully shared. As we think about the importance of interconnectedness reflected in relationships, we conclude that congregation leadership is better thought of in terms of webs of influence than chains of command.

## Diversity: For All of Us Are One

Diversity is a consequence of the process of evolution. Our biologist consultant said, "Evolution is the underriding principle of all biology. If you don't understand evolution, you don't understand how life works." Evolution leads to greater and greater diversity at all biological levels. Diversity is critical to the well-being of an ecological unit. Take the human, for example. According to our biologist, one of the most diverse systems in our bodies is the immune system, used to fight diseases. If we do not have great diversity within our own system, we cannot survive. We know that some babies born without this diversity are subject to any disease that is around and are confined to living in germ-free bubbles. In this book we will explore what encouraging diversity means for communities of faith. However, we understand that evolutional biology has often been misused to further a political agenda—as happened with the concept of social Darwinism. Hitler's attempt to form a superior Aryan race at the expense of the Jews and others is a classic example of the grave danger of social Darwinism. In turn, we know that we have to be deeply cautious about applying biological concepts such as "natural selection" to social communities such as the church.

## Process: An Invitation to Adventure

This scientific concept states that processes are as important as things. People have long thought of "substance" as a primary category and action as secondary, which has led to "an underlying assumption that things are somehow more 'real' than processes. And things became identified with mass, and processes with energy."[19] Sir Isaac Newton distinguished between mass and energy. An example of our privileging things (mass) over processes (energy) is that most congregations are convinced that it is more important for their well-being to use church monies to build beautiful church buildings than to establish a preschool for disadvantaged children or provide resources and teachers for English as a second language.

However, within the scientific community, the primacy of mass over energy changed with Albert Einstein, who demonstrated in his special theory of relativity (1905) that ultimately matter and energy are identical.[20] If we ought no longer to make a rigid distinction between things and processes, if processes are not less important than things, our rethinking will naturally cause a change in how we conceive of a leader's role and what takes top priority for the leader.

### The Center: Where Trust Prevails

After we spend a chapter on each of the five insights from the philosophy of science about the way the world works, we examine the crucial issue of trust. Throughout this book, we are cautious about making direct causal links between science and leadership in a congregation. However, by means of these analogies, we offer readers not another list of strategies to be an effective leader, but rather a different worldview—and a different way of thinking about the idea of leadership itself. If the principles of science we discuss describe the way the world works, then clergy and lay leaders whose insights and behaviors reflect these principles will not only think differently about leadership but will discover a different way of leading, one that will enable them to most faithfully and effectively fulfill their vocation to serve God's mission in the world.

# 1

## *Information*

## *God's New Thing*

"***M****OM, STOP! TMI! TOO MUCH INFORMATION!" FOURTEEN*-year-old Tyler signaled time out, pleading with his mother to abandon her detailed recounting of plans for her father's upcoming birthday party. "Mom, I don't need to know all that stuff!" he protested.

How often we feel as overwhelmed by information as Tyler did. "TMI!" we want to shout to the universe. Daily we are awash in opinion poll results, stock market analyses, and demographic trends data. Twenty-four-hour news services regurgitate the same salacious story about the latest celebrity scandal after each commercial break. A simple search on Google produces 6,570,000 hits. We would need a pickup truck to hold all the paper required to print the information stored on a one-gigabyte flash drive, a device smaller than an adult's thumb. A family of four depends on a personal digital assistant to manage its conflicting schedules.

Given the amount of information each of us encounters in a day, how disconcerting, then, to read Margaret Wheatley's observation:

> For a system to remain alive . . . information must be continually generated. If there is nothing new, or if the information merely confirms what already is, then the result will be death. Closed systems wind down and decay. . . . The source of life is new information—novelty—ordered into new structures. We need to have information coursing through our systems, disturbing the peace, imbuing everything it touches with the possibility of new life. We

need, therefore, to develop new approaches to information—not management but encouragement, not control but genesis.[1]

Even more distressing to those who think we already have access to—and are even accosted by—too much information, the "cusp" between order and chaos is "the place that fosters further growth and creativity," observes Carol Rausch Albright.[2] Philosophers, psychologists, neuroscientists, and others tell us that humans naturally seek to order their world. As Harvard psychologist and educator Robert Kegan notes, "What an organism does . . . is organize."[3] The prospect of too much disorder, even in the service of growth and creativity, makes us uneasy. Before we become too alarmed by the notion of a universe run amok and inundated with information, though, let's step back and ask, what is "information"?

## *The Theory*

Information, says Wheatley, lies at the heart of life. British anthropologist and linguist Gregory Bateson says, "Information is a difference which makes a difference," and cybernetics expert Stafford Beer says, "Information is that which changes us."[4] We tend to think of information as "things"—little bundles of reality that are consistent over time and that we can perceive and manage by some means. For babies, information is closely related to experience. When Mommy plays peek-a-boo and disappears behind the blanket, Mommy is not hiding; she is gone. As children develop cognitively, they begin to understand that sometimes there is more to the world than what they perceive through their senses. When the three-year-old sees her mother leave the house in the morning, the child understands Mommy is going to work. The child does not think her mother ceases to exist for nine or ten hours just because Mommy is out of sight.

Adults are generally willing to accept as fact much that they have not personally witnessed—that petroleum is trapped between layers of rock beneath the earth's surface, that a gallon of water flowing down the Mississippi River will eventually end up in the Gulf of Mexico, that the earth revolves around the sun, that sodium and chloride ions bond to create the salt we sprinkle on our scrambled eggs.

Sophisticated scientists posit phenomena that may never be directly observed by anyone. Superstring theory, for example, has been proposed by some physicists to unify known natural forces—such as gravity, electromagnetic fields, and various nuclear forces—with a single set of mathematical equations. No one has seen or is likely to see this theorized "string," but the theory may prove useful in explaining a good many puzzles in atomic physics.

Information is more than facts, whether directly apprehended or inferred, however—more than a "thing" we can get our hands around, move from place to place, and expect to remain unchanged.[5] In the mid-twentieth century, information theorist Claude Shannon conceived of information as "the description of the way the world goes round: the shape assumed by substances, the sequence assumed by processes, and the interactions among substances and processes."[6] Information itself is a dynamic, changing element that, according to Wheatley, "All life uses . . . to organize itself into form. A living being is not a stable structure, but a continuous *process* of organizing information."[7] As you read this book, your body's form at both the cellular and systemic levels is constantly changing, providing nourishment and managing waste. But "you" continue to exist. What endures and evolves over time is not the form but the processes.[8]

This understanding of information as process is challenging to nonscientists, who tend to view information as static. Nonscientists also consider the claim that something is "scientific fact" the gold standard of certainty about how the world works. Scientists themselves see their work—their interpretations of information—as always provisional, however, and remain open to the possibility that additional information will yield more accurate understandings. Information itself consists of descriptions, and science is not a repository of "true facts," but a method for rigorously testing and refining those descriptions. Writers for the National Academy of Sciences elaborate:

> In science, explanations are limited to those based on observations and experiments that can be substantiated by other scientists.

> Explanations that cannot be based on empirical evidence are not part
> of science.... Scientists can never be sure that a given explanation is
> complete and final. Some hypotheses advanced by scientists turn out
> to be incorrect when tested by further observations and experiments.
> Yet many scientific explanations have been so thoroughly tested and
> confirmed that they are held with great confidence.[9]

We can find many examples across the centuries of explanations that
were once viewed as accurate and later abandoned. Once upon a time,
before the scientific age, people thought the male of a species carried
a tiny but complete being in his sperm cells. When sperm was depos-
ited in a female's womb, it was supposed, that minute being grew to
become a baby. Now researchers are mapping the entire human ge-
nome, currently believed to consist of twenty thousand to twenty-five
thousand genes. As the scientific era dawned, diseases were believed to
be caused by spontaneous generation—until, amid great controversy,
the germ theory was developed. Even Niels Bohr's model of the atom
as a miniature solar system, a theory for which he received a Nobel
Prize in 1922, was long ago negated by particle physics.[10]

What is helpful for congregation leaders is not scientific method
itself but the understanding that information is (1) provisional (the
best description we can come up with for now) and therefore subject
to change, and (2) about both substance and process, as well as the
interactions between them. Further, in an open system—a web of
relationships among elements that continuously interacts with its
environment—information moves freely within the system itself and
between the system and its surroundings.

## *Freedom and Order*

As important as it is for information to move freely, some dependable
laws or order is also required if a system is to be productive. Albright
argues that the universe currently seems to function with a combination of freedom and order. "This arrangement allows . . . for change
and development and richness of life."[11] As we noted above, Albright
believes this place between extreme control and complete lack of order

is the creative edge of a system. When out of insecurity we attempt to impose too much order on a system, we lose that creative edge, a birthing place for information. But when we are willing to live with a combination of freedom and order, we see the greatest potential for growth. We make way for new information and the possibility of new life.

When information in a system is free, the system is well nourished and agile, and consequently responsive, able to adapt. Free-flowing information makes a system more stable, because based on the information it notices, the system responds to its environment, thus preserving itself and ensuring that it is able to carry out its purposes. Wheatley notes, "If a system has the capacity to process information, to notice and respond, the system possesses the quality of *intelligence*."[12] Because each description holds within it the possibility of new information, a system in which information is continuously generated and flows freely has the potential for great growth and vitality.

Increasing the amount of information in a system is not an absolute good, however. On the cellular level in biological systems, uncontrolled growth is called cancer. Cancer cells are distinctive in that, whereas most cells divide a fixed number of times (approximately fifty) before they die, cancer cells can divide until the host organism itself dies, and it is the uncontrolled growth of cells (mitosis) that ultimately kills the organism. What keeps a system from generating so much information that it kills itself? Several concepts together help us answer this question.

- *Autopoiesis* means literally "self-creation" (from the Greek: *auto* ["self"] + *poiesis* ["creation, production"]). Wheatley explains, "Autopoiesis is life's fundamental process for creating and renewing itself, for growth and change. A living system is a network of processes in which every process contributes to all other processes."[13] Whereas a machine in a metal-stamping plant might produce parts for cars, living cells produce more living cells. Cells and other living systems do not self-create in isolation, however. They must be in constant communication with their environment. In other words, information must flow freely to and from the system, as well as within the system itself—

meaning in a church that it is not healthy to keep the information loop closed, restricted to the congregation itself. The congregation must also always be communicating with and receiving input from the rest of the world. The notion of autopoiesis is often associated with that of self-organization.

- *Self-organization* is a process in which an open system reorganizes itself to deal with new information. Open systems are adaptive and resilient, rather than rigid and unchanging. Such a system "is not locked into any one form but instead is capable of organizing information in the structure that best suits the present need."[14] Self-organizing systems do not merely cope with new information; they actively seek it, because this information tells the system how it might need to change in order to survive and grow.[15] This phenomenon was first observed in physics, but it can also be seen in numerous other disciplines in both the natural and social sciences. Developmental psychologists observe that whereas several two-year-olds in a room will play side by side, by age five, small groups of children work together—without adults' direction—to create and act out scenarios and coordinate games that require taking turns and sharing. We see the principle at work in congregations when interest groups form—without input or approval from the board, a committee, or staff members—to study a book or conduct a service project.

- *Feedback loops*, first explored in the 1940s as an element of communications theory, are processes that allow a system to monitor what is happening within the system and its environment and to make changes required to maintain the system. Self-reference occurs whenever a system loops back on itself and describes some aspect of its own form or structure. A negative or regulatory feedback loop tends to keep a system on track, while a positive or amplifying feedback loop signals a need to change.[16] Systems use both types of loops to manage information and self-organize. The most common example of a negative feedback loop is the thermostat, which is designed to keep temperatures constant. A shrieking sound system is an example of positive feedback, sometimes also called "amplifying" feedback. Clearly something needs to change when the sound is going round and round![17] Congregations use various reflection and evaluation processes, sometimes involving someone from outside the system, to help them stay on track as well as to identify practices that are interfering with their mission and ministry.

- *Identity* is the coherence of a system that is able to maintain an internal order over time. Identity is defined in relation to other systems, allowing a system to determine what does and does not belong to the system (what is "meaningful"), and is closely related to purpose. Essential to identity is *self-reference*, the process by which a system changes, as Wheatley explains, "in such a way that it remains consistent with itself." Wheatley continues, "Change is never random; the system will not take off in bizarre new directions. Paradoxically, it is the system's need to maintain itself that may lead it to become something new and different. A living system changes in order to preserve itself."[18] In other words, change creates stability in a system that has a clear identity. A congregation challenged to address changing neighborhood demographics might study Scripture, the creeds and confessional documents central to its tradition, and its own constitution and by-laws, initially clarifying its identity as it prepares to respond to change in the wider community.

So, what keeps a system from generating so much information that it kills itself? These concepts—autopoiesis, self-organization, feed-back loops, and identity or self-reference—together show us that a system tends to use information in a way that reinforces the system. Even new information from outside the system is processed in a way that strengthens the system itself, which is why we do not need to be afraid of freedom in a system. Biologists Francisco Varela and Humberto Maturana describe this phenomenon in the maxim "You can never direct a living system. You can only disturb it."[19] An important implication of these principles is that living systems are always in re-lationship with other systems; they cannot function in isolation and remain alive. Without constant access to new information, a system will weaken and die. Unlike a cancer cell, which reproduces without regard to the needs, function, or identity of the system it has invaded, information nourishes a system. An isolated system, one that does not interact with its environment (and potentially change its environment, a topic we will explore in chapter 3), will eventually starve to death. For a system to thrive, therefore, it must always remain open to new information.

## *Scripture*

How do these ideas about information fit with biblical understandings of the way the world works? The commonalities are striking. Particularly fascinating is the way Hebrew and Greek understandings of "word" parallel current thinking about "information." In each notion, we encounter both substance and process. In Hebrew, *dabar*, most often translated "word," is thought by some scholars to come from a root meaning "to speak." But *dabar* conveys a sense of both the act of speaking and the thing spoken. A word does not simply describe action and thing, however. Rather, it does what it says. *Dabar* is both substance and process! We first see this dual meaning in Genesis, where God, by speaking, calls the whole universe into being. "God said, 'Let there be light'; and there was light" (Gen. 1:3). From light to humankind, God spoke, and it was so. The prophet Isaiah attests to the power of God's word:

> For as the rain and the snow come down from heaven,
>     and do not return there until they have watered the earth,
> making it bring forth and sprout,
>     giving seed to the sower and bread to the eater,
> so shall my word be that goes out from my mouth;
>     it shall not return to me empty,
> but it shall accomplish that which I purpose,
>     and succeed in the thing for which I sent it. (Isa. 55:10-11)

In the centuries when the Old Testament was written, even words spoken by humans were understood to have power, however. Blessings and curses were thought to change the course of human events. So when Isaac mistakenly blessed Jacob, rather than Esau (Gen. 27:32-38), Isaac could not simply "undo" the blessing or offer Esau a similar blessing. A path had been laid—one that Jacob alone, not Esau, would walk. False prophets, those who spoke words that would please their sponsors rather than God's word, were viewed as dangerous because they unleashed forces contrary to God's intentions. King Jehoshaphat attempted to shop around for a prophet who would prophesy, and thereby bring about, events in his favor (1 Kings 22:5-38). A true prophet like Balaam obeyed God's command, insisting, "The word God puts in my mouth, that is what I must say" (Num. 22:38). Words were not simply labels; to speak a word was to change the world.

In the New Testament, *logos* (again, most often translated "word") has multiple meanings, including the Old Testament law, a particular passage from the Old Testament, God's will or purpose, the word preached by Jesus, and the Christian message. Of most interest for this discussion, however, is the use of *logos* as a title for Christ in the prologue of John (John 1:1-14). "The Word became flesh" means that "through the life, teaching, actions, and death of the man Jesus a new revelation of God has been given, different in kind from that made through the prophets."[20] Understood in light of the Old Testament use of *dabar*, the image would have made sense to John's audience. God spoke the Word, Jesus Christ, bringing him into being and setting into motion irreversible, world-altering processes.

We see another connection between scriptural and scientific views about the way the world works in the unfolding of creation. "In the beginning when God created the heavens and the earth, the earth was a formless void" (Gen. 1:1). Without equating this "formless void" to the nonlinear systems described by mathematicians and physicists, we recognize that in both realms lies great generativity. In the midst of unbounded emptiness and through the voice of God, the substances and processes of the universe were unleashed. More remarkable, however, creation continues to this day and into the future. The God of history speaks again and again, so that long after light was separated from darkness and the waters from dry land, the universe teems with newness. Yahweh declared through the prophet Isaiah:

I am the LORD, that is my name. . . .
See, the former things have come to pass,
    And new things I now declare;
before they spring forth,
    I tell you of them. (Isa. 42:8-9)

And now, in these last days, Jesus Christ, the firstborn of all creation (Col. 1:15), points us to the day when the whole creation will be set free (Rom. 8:21). When God whispered Jesus Christ into the still night skies over Bethlehem, a multitude of the heavenly host sang out, "Glory to God in the highest heaven!" Their hymn was all out of proportion to what normally happens when a sound is uttered—or a baby is born. Unpredictably, Jesus's mission, to inaugurate the reign of God, grew like a mustard seed, "the smallest of all the seeds, but when it has grown it is the greatest of shrubs and becomes a tree, so that the birds of the air come and make nests in its branches" (Matt. 13:32). Slowly, a new order was revealed, until finally, in Christ, "everything old has passed away; see, everything has become new!" (2 Cor. 5:17).

From the beginning, creation has been more than a teeming, lumpy mud soup. After God made the earth and the heavens, planted the garden, and fashioned the animals and birds, God brought every creature to the man "to see what he would call them" (Gen. 2:19). Thus, each was given an identity, a concept that continues to be significant throughout Scripture. The people of God are repeatedly called to be faithful to their distinct identity as God's chosen ones—to be holy, set apart. Repeatedly, Israel is declared or called to be a holy nation (see, for example, Exod. 19:5-6; Deut. 7:6-8; 14:2; Isa. 61-63; Ezek. 36:22-27). The First Letter of Peter, possibly addressed to leaders of churches throughout Asia Minor, declares that the church (including Gentiles) is the true heir of God's covenant with Israel: "You are a chosen race, a royal priesthood, a holy nation, God's own people" (2:9). Other passages emphasize the continuity between Israel and the church, while still setting both apart from the world. The third chapter of Colossians, for example, is an exhortation on the Christian life, and in the middle of this advice, we read, "In that renewal there is no longer Greek and Jew, circumcised and uncircumcised, barbarian, Scythian, slave and free, but Christ is all and in all!" Then the writer immediately addresses his audience: "As God's chosen ones, holy and beloved" (Col. 3:11-12a; see also Rom. 10:12 and 1 Cor. 1:24).

This survey of Scripture is not intended to prove that the biblical writers understood information and its role in living systems long before scientists began to articulate the concepts. Nor is it intended to suggest that "if the Bible says it," the science must be right. Rather, the point is that the ideas we are exploring in this book are part of a broad, ancient-modern wisdom about how the world works, an understanding that can help us reflect on our own roles in the systems of which we are a part. So we now turn our attention to a system that has baffled and delighted God's people through the ages and around the world—the community of faith, the congregation.

## Identity in Congregations

Among the ideas related to the role of information discussed above, one seems especially promising for congregations. We believe the concept of identity, the coherence of a system that is able to maintain an internal order over time, can deepen our understanding of congregations and how to lead them most effectively. Wheatley points us to the power of this concept:

> The work of any team or organization needs to start with a clear sense of what they are trying to accomplish and how they want to behave. . . . Once this clarity is established, people will use it as their lens to interpret information, surprises, experience. They will be able to figure out what and how to do their work. . . . We need to evoke contributions through freedom, trusting that people can make sense of information because they know their jobs, and they know the organizational or team purpose.[21]

Congregations, like other systems, thrive when they are clear about their identity—who they are and why they exist. Such churches are agile and responsive and at the same time stable and appropriately ordered. Information flows freely within the congregation and between the system and its environment, and the congregation, possessing a strong sense of self-knowledge, uses the information to grow stronger, making changes that are consistent with itself. Leaders and members need not fear that new information and the changes the congregation makes in response to that information will destroy the congregation.

Wheatley draws on her experiences with public school systems to demonstrate how a system's identity—or lack of a clear identity—functions. She notes that school systems often are not really systems with a shared identity but rather are artificial entities with boundaries drawn by someone else. She continues:

> They are not systems because they do not arise from a core of shared beliefs about the purpose of public education [we might substitute "the congregation"]. In the absence of shared beliefs and desires, people are not motivated to seek out one another and develop relationships. Instead, they inhabit the same organizational and community space without weaving together mutually sustaining relationships. They co-exist by defining clear boundaries, creating respectful and disrespectful distances, developing self-protective behaviors, and using power politics to get what they want.[22]

Too many congregations are like the school districts Wheatley describes, never articulating and living out an identity or making clear that this identity encompasses the core beliefs and values of this church.

## Identity in the Early Church

Some writers about congregational life say that defining a core identity is easy, because the Bible, through the words of Jesus, Paul, and others, tells us what the church's identity is. The truth is that Christian leaders have fought throughout the history of the church over the purpose of the church. In the church's infancy, the apostles and elders debated whether Gentiles must be circumcised to be saved. The account of the Jerusalem Council in Acts 15 is an excellent example of how a living system successfully deals with new information. Jesus's followers, a fellowship of Jews who had encountered the Messiah and were eager to spread the good news that the reign of God was fulfilled, learned that Gentiles were joining their company. Some in the community were disturbed by this new information.

Rather than closing ranks to keep the Gentiles out, however, the church's leaders opened themselves to that creative space between rigid order ("We've always done it this way") and complete disorder (perhaps fighting to the death of the unfolding church). The leaders came together and were reminded of two important aspects of the community's identity. To carry out God's purpose—to spread the good news and make new disciples—(1) God had chosen Peter to witness to the Gentiles (Acts 15:7), and (2) in the past, God had "looked favorably on the Gentiles" (vv. 14ff.). The church's leaders then fed some new information into their system: God "had opened a door of faith for the Gentiles" (14:27), demonstrating that God made no distinction between Jew and Gentile (15:9). The church responded positively, viewing the information about God's actions in this situation as consistent with the community's identity, and concluded, "We should not trouble those Gentiles who are turning to God" (v. 19). The church moved *toward* the new information that was disturbing it—with unanticipated, explosive results!

The church's identity changed after that assembly. No longer did the church understand itself as an exclusively Jewish fellowship, for example. At the same time, as a result of this conflict and the new information the community processed, the church became clearer about its purpose. Circumcision would not be required, but to maintain the church's identity as a people set apart by God, Gentile Christians would "abstain from what has been sacrificed to idols and from blood and from what is strangled and from fornication" (Acts 15:29), practices common among Gentiles of the day. By changing, the church remained true to itself and grew stronger, rather than starving and eventually destroying itself.

## Struggling for Identity Today

The Jerusalem Council was not the last time the church struggled to deal with new information—or even to clarify its identity. The Gospel and Our Culture Network (GOCN) identifies itself as "a network of

Christian leaders from a wide array of churches and organizations, who are working together on the frontier of the missionary encounter of the gospel with North American assumptions, perspectives, preferences and practices."[23] A GOCN study group offered this definition of the church: "The missional church represents God in the encounter between God and human nature. It exists not because of human goals or desires, but as a result of God's creating and saving work in the world. It is a visible manifestation of how the good news of Jesus Christ is present in human life and transforms human culture to reflect more faithfully God's intention for creation."[24]

In general terms, we authors agree with the thrust of this definition, but we also argue against some of its language. We have a keen sense that sin operates within the church—in every believer—as well as outside the church. Therefore, our claims about the church's capacity to transform human culture are more modest that this study group's. We caution that if the church, as a missional community, is a window to God, we must remember we look through stained glass rather than clear panes. If we authors disagree with one aspect of one description of the church's identity, a statement for which we generally have great sympathy, you can imagine the disagreements about the church's identity across the wider Christian spectrum.

Even if all church bodies worldwide could agree on the church's identity, however, the resultant definition would still be a long way from the lived reality of Christian congregations. A congregation's identity is found not only in statements articulated by a congregation's leaders and members, but in the everyday patterns of life that make each congregation unique. Often, as in our personal lives, what we say we are as a congregation is far different from what we do. However, the situation is actually worse than this: most congregations do not even have an articulated identity and are not aware of this fact. Our experience, as we authors investigate and study many congregations, is that even among congregations that have developed a mission statement, many have no articulated identity. At some point in the past a committee of congregational leaders developed a mission statement that fit all the recommended criteria. It was developed with input from the entire community, and it was short and easy to understand, remember, and say. But before long, that statement was gathering dust in a file cabinet. Bill will never forget the pastor who said to him, "Oh yeah, we have one [a mission statement] someplace. I don't remember what it says. Let me rummage in my desk for a bit, and I'll find it." (In his defense, the mission statement had been developed during his predecessor's tenure.)

Another challenge to clarifying a congregation's identity is that many congregations have existed for decades and sometimes centuries, so their identity, articulated or not, is multilayered and complex and therefore difficult to describe in a few words. In these cases, the identity derives not just from tradition (the biblical and theological confessions of the whole church) but also from accretions of local traditions that make each congregation different from its neighbors, even neighboring congregations from the same denomination. In fact, some Christians who write about revolutionizing our way of being church so congregations can reach people in our postmodern world are willing to address only new congregations and not those with long histories. For example, Australian church planters Michael Frost and Alan Hirsch write, "Right up front we want to confess our belief that the planting of new, culturally diverse, missional communities is the best way forward for the church that views itself in a missional context. . . . While some established churches can be revitalized, success seems to be rare from our experience and perspective."[25] We authors are not ready to write off established churches in such a cavalier fashion, but Frost and Hirsch certainly point to the difficulty of naming, examining, and changing identity in an established congregation.

## *The Intelligent Congregation*

As difficult as it might be for a congregation to clearly articulate its identity, the task is essential to a faith community's well-being. Systems require a clear identity for stability, and this stability in turn "helps shelter it from many of the demands from the environment" and "enables it to develop in ways of its own choosing, not just as a fearful reactant."[26] Identity is so central to the way we function in the world (after all, God asked Adam to name all the animals in the garden) that without realizing the specific role identity plays in living systems, people will ascribe to a church an identity that makes sense to them. We hear clues to that identity in the simplest descriptions: "I belong to Tall Steeple Presbyterian, where Rev. MacMillan was pastor for forty years." "We go to Tight Knit Lutheran—the church my great-grand-parents helped build." "My parents are buried in the cemetery next to Our Lady of Determination, and our kids go to the new high school there." "Well, we're so busy we don't make it to church very often, but when we do go, we like Catchy Community Church. They have a retreat center, an assisted living facility, and a great summer camp!"

Based on an intuition that identity is important to a church, lead-ers and members of churches that are hazy about their identity might attempt to create one. A member of a small urban congregation Beth once served proposed that the church develop a logo to help attract at-tention in the neighborhood. This longtime member thought the logo should include a church mouse because "they're cute, like we are—and besides, we have mice." People also signal that they understand the significance of identity by the way they react to perceived threats to that identity. Instinctively, they will "batten the hatches," "circle the wagons," "close the barn door"—grabbing at every possible strategy (and cliché!) to "save themselves." The way living systems function in realms outside the church, however, suggests these instincts—to con-coct an identity out of the handiest ingredients or to preserve a fragile one by any means—might be counterproductive. If congregations are living systems, and we believe they are, such self-preservation strate-gies might bring about a congregation's demise, rather than increase its vitality. So what is a congregation to do?

A system's identity grows out of more than a logo or even a so-phisticated, comprehensive marketing campaign. Identity, as Wheatley says, "comes from a deepening centre, a clarity about who it is, what it needs, what is required to survive in its environment."[27] Identity creates stability in a system. That stability, in turn, begins with freely flowing information—the more the better. Recall also that intelligence is the capacity to notice and respond to information. So in order to form a clear, sturdy identity, congregations need to become more intelligent. They need access to lots of information, and they need to learn how to process that information according to the principles all living systems follow:

- Information is the nourishment a system requires to grow.
- An adaptive, resilient system seeks out new information and allows information to flow freely within the system and between the system and its environment to maintain its identity.
- A system uses identity, or self-reference, to organize information—both to filter out information that does not reinforce the system and to accept information that enhances it, sometimes by alerting the system to the need for change.
- What emerges when information moves freely and is processed through self-reference is "an integrated system that can resist most demands for change at the global level because there is so much internal motion" but that will change when needed to preserve itself.[28]

Wheatley describes information as the basic ingredient of the universe. She also bemoans the ways we tend to mistreat it:

> We haven't been interested in newness. We've taken disturbances and fluctuations and averaged them together to give us comfortable statistics. Our training has been to look for large numbers, important trends, major variances. . . . We struggle to smooth out the differences, conform to standards, measure up. . . . Even when we do notice new information, we too often rush to kill it off. . . . We value quick decisions over wise ones.[29]

A congregation concerned primarily with protecting itself against supposed threats, whether internal or external, might also limit the amount or minimize the significance of information from outside the system, stifle the flow of information within the system so that only a few people have access to it, or focus on implications of information for other congregations or organizations, rather than for itself. Congregations that insist God calls them to be faithful, not successful (with the implication that they therefore do not need to be concerned about what is going on "out there"), communities where only a small circle of people are invited to help discern the congregation's vocation to its neighbors, churches that insist they are exceptions to broader trends in the church and society are likely hampering the flow of information in the system. In all these ways, congregations that intend to bolster themselves end up more vulnerable—undernourished, internally incoherent, and therefore unable to recognize or respond to disturbing information from the environment.

Such a congregation is like a fifty-year-old cottonwood tree. It grew quickly, achieving impressive girth and height. The majestic tree is drought resistant, and its wide canopy provides shade and shelter for birds and four-legged creatures. But in spite of these attributes, a cottonwood is what foresters call "weak wooded"—more susceptible to wood decay than most other slower-growing trees. Wind, heavy snow, or even water saturation can cause a decaying limb or an entire tree with decay to structurally fail.[30] Of course, a cottonwood cannot "choose" how it processes nutrients or responds to its environment. The point is that cottonwoods are generally magnificent trees, but because they are weak wooded, they often harbor disease and are vulnerable to challenges a slower-growing tree can survive. A congregation that either lacks a clear, robust identity or attempts to protect its identity by impeding the flow of information among its own members or with its environment, while it may (though will not necessarily) look spectacular, is going to be a "weak wooded" congregation.

## *Growing in Intelligence*

So how does a congregation become intelligent? As we have been saying, the ability to articulate identity is essential. Wheatley describes identity as "the lens of values, traditions, history, dreams, experience, competencies, [and] culture."[31] A congregation will not thrive if all it has is a lens, however. A congregation needs to be well nourished. It needs a constantly expanding array of data, views, and interpretations to make sense of the world.[32] It needs lots of truthful, meaningful, potent information, information that is "different, disconfirming, and filled with enough newness to disturb the system into wise solutions."[33] And how does a congregation get new information? By inviting people—both leaders and members—to look for it. By making new connections, journeying into other disciplines or places, and forming active, collegial networks. By forming ongoing circles of exchange where information is not just accumulated by individuals, but is willingly shared.[34] Congregations need to seek novelty and deliberately disturb the peace.

A congregation that wants to become more intelligent might invite an undocumented worker from El Salvador to talk during the Sunday education hour about what life is like for her. A church board might spend an hour imagining what could happen if the congregation gave away 15 rather than 5 percent of its income. A group of members might worship with a different congregation one week each month and report on their experience in a joint meeting of the worship and evangelism committees. The deacons or elders of a congregation might get in touch with every family or individual who stopped attending church over the past year—not to drag them back to church but simply to listen to their story about leaving the congregation. Each of these conversations has the potential to produce insights and shake a congregation's preconceptions about itself and others.

The role of information in vital systems explains why one of the first steps of a well-conceived congregation planning process is to gather information. The congregation creates a timeline of its history, noting significant dates, players, victories, and crises in the past. It examines unspoken traditions and norms, clues to the congregation's culture, and artifacts—documents, photographs, and the like. Planners explore the building and grounds; pore over demographic data about members, visitors, and constituents; interview neighbors and community experts; and conduct surveys about the congregation's internal and external resources and needs. Throughout these studies, leaders listen carefully to discern the hopes and dreams of the congregation and those it serves. The point of this phase is simply to gather information. Congregation consultants Gil Rendle and Alice Mann advise, "The leaders' role is to structure the conversation, to ask the conversation partners continuously what would be helpful next, and to keep the process open to God and to the actual setting and context of the people."[35] Leaders do not need to worry about steering process but do need to keep it moving—and to help everyone pay attention.

Wheatley's guidance about ways to seek information suggests that intelligent congregations expect planners to look beyond the obvious for information. In such faith communities, people talk with

Sunday school students and the homebound—not only the people who serve on boards and committees. They interview the owner of the cafe on the main drag, the manager of the service station at the truck stop on the highway, and the guy who has been mixing paint at the neighborhood hardware store for the past thirty years—not only the local school board members or the mayor. They study the activity calendar for the city sports dome and schedules for local commuter trains—not just U.S. Census data. They walk down streets they usually drive along and try to imagine what their impressions would be if this were their first visit to this church, neighborhood, or community. Congregations that grow in intelligence by exercising such unbridled curiosity when planning can also learn to operate this way in every arena of congregational life—worship, education, fellowship, outreach, and support.

Second, congregations become intelligent by working with information, as Wheatley says, "the same way life does."[36] They establish fluid, open boundaries and easy access to information. They learn to live with uncertainty, ambivalence, and ambiguity—the ground from which information is formed. Here we meet a challenge, however: these things make us anxious, so we shield ourselves from them and their effects, holding on to the myth that prediction and control are possible.[37] A spiritual director we interviewed commented, "How often people say, 'I work with a group that funnels out a little bit of information, believing that the person who has the most of it has the most power.'"

Leaders of a congregation with which Beth is familiar do not make announcements about congregational goings-on at Sunday worship, based on their belief that reports about upcoming events, invitations to participate in work or study groups, and the like interfere with the congregation's primary task: worship. Rather than include information about such activities in the congregation's weekly newsletter, however, the leaders either post notices on bulletin boards outside the church office or make announcements at the beginning of the adult fellowship and education hour, typically attended by fewer than 10 percent of the people at worship. Leaders reason that if people really want to know what is going on in the congregation, they can read the posted information and attend the adult class! Although the leaders might not intend to limit the number of people who know what is going on in the congregation's life, they effectively control the flow of information—and prevent anyone from upsetting "their" system. Few people know enough about the community to be able to contribute time, skills, or expertise, offer another perspective, or raise questions. The congregation's worship attendance and financial status are quite stable. Is the congregation vital as it could be? Probably not.

Of course, the leaders of this congregation are not the only church leaders who so effectively limit the flow of information. Beth knows the leaders well enough to be confident that they are not malicious power mongers. But how can they—how do we—deal with the anxiety they feel when their sense of control begins to slip? Recalling the importance of both freedom and order for growth in systems is helpful.

## Information and Identity

In a system that can be described using Newtonian physics, a system such as an automobile, the whole is equal to the sum of the parts. Given appropriate tools and expertise, we could reach into the vehicle's past, dismantling it into a pile of parts and retracing the steps used to assemble it. We could also predict how the car will perform in the future—how long it will take to get it moving sixty miles per hour, how likely it is to tip over going around a sharp curve, and what the stopping distance will be on a dry, straight road.

In a living organism, the parts are even more intricately related than the parts in a Newtonian system, and the whole that emerges from those parts is greater than the sum of the parts. Such a living system is also not sequential, so behavior cannot be predicted by examining simple cause-and-effect processes. No one would predict that by putting a seed into a pot of earth, setting it in the sun, and regularly watering it, we would end up with a marigold. No one would expect after watching a flock of geese roaming and awkwardly nibbling grass in the city park that the birds could take off and fly hundreds of miles in a graceful, ever-changing, but sustainable V-formation. Similar surprising phenomena—"wholes" much greater than the sum of their "parts"—have been noted in fields such as economics, architecture and urban growth, and political science.

As leaders and members of congregations, we can deal with our anxiety about the uncertain future by stepping back and focusing our attention on what we do know. The church in every place and time, including our own faith community as it gathers on Sunday mornings, is the fruit of God's marvelous deeds. Every member, though unique, is connected to the others, and what we are together as the body of Christ is far greater than who we members are individually. Out of a sense of our connection with the great cloud of witnesses throughout the ages and our interrelatedness in the present, we can approach the future without anxiety, secure in the knowledge that God, who brought all life into being, is working in us both individually and collectively to create a new thing.

From this perspective, we can seek out and welcome information from a wide range of likely and unlikely sources, finding nourishment wherever it is available. We can embrace the free movement of information as a process essential to the congregation's growth. Recognizing that information and identity work together in a living system, we can be confident that a congregation will change to preserve itself, given clues it gathers about changes in its environment. And trusting that the mechanisms at work in all living systems—autopoiesis (self-creation), self-organization, and feedback loops—also function in congregations, we can get out of the way as fellow members draw on the information coursing throughout the system and together create and recreate new ministries—and a stabler and yet more vital community. As all of us see, order, and respond to the information available both within the congregation and in our neighborhood and the global environment, the congregation's clear identity will guide us. At the same time, we well-informed decision makers will help to further strengthen and clarify that identity.

Readers might hear in this scenario echoes of the "permission-giving church" promoted by congregation consultant William Easum and others. We authors do not agree with all aspects of Easum's assessment about how the church has functioned in the past or conclusions about the shape of the future church. We see in his work, however, a strategy for organizing ministries that is consistent with our understanding of information as "the description of the way the world goes round" and identity as "the coherence of a system that is able to maintain an internal order over time." We think Easum would also affirm the need for lots of free-flowing information to create a vital and stable congregation. For example, he writes that a permission-giving church "is clear about its values and mission, and also gives permission for each person to live out those values and mission through the exercise of their spiritual gifts."[38] Easum also offers a helpful analogy for permission-giving churches that fits our understanding of the way information, identity, and freedom function in a system: "Permission-giving churches are more like a soccer or a basketball team. All of the players understand the game plan, but on the playing field or court, it is up to each player to make split-second decisions as to what to do. The coach has trained them and given them a game plan, but each of them is free to make decisions as the ball is moved up and down the field or court."[39] The players know what game they are playing—that they are not geared up for lacrosse or polo. But within that system, the players and rules—the substances and processes of the game— function with great freedom to produce unpredictable outcomes. Such systems are sometimes called "nimble" or "agile."

## Making a Difference

Several years ago Beth served on the board of an inner-city congregation (we will call it "Grace Lutheran Church") where she and her husband were members. Grace had been established in 1909 to serve English-speaking Lutherans, an alternative to the many area Lutheran churches where German, Norwegian, or Swedish was spoken. The community surrounding Grace was white and middle-class, but beginning in the 1970s, the neighborhood demographics began to change, and the pins on the map showing where Grace's members lived gradually took on the doughnut shape typical of city churches. Now the church is surrounded by a large "hole" where only a few members live and, further out, a ring of suburbs, exurbs, and small towns as far as fifty miles away, from which members regularly drive for worship, attracted by the congregation's elegant, formal worship service with nationally recognized musical offerings.

Still, Grace Lutheran has worked hard in recent decades to stay connected to its neighborhood. When the Sunday school shrank, the congregation turned over several rooms in its education wing to the area Women, Infants, and Children (WIC) Program and a federally funded health clinic for women and children. A neighborhood ministries coordinator manages a variety of programs, some staffed by members. Located on a major bus route and a short block from a second major route, the church is ideally situated for people who do not own a car but need the services Grace offers, and these programs are central to Grace Lutheran's identity as a congregation.

When Beth was on the church's board, a large, rundown, two-story duplex (each story contained an apartment) next door to the church went up for sale. The owner offered the property to Grace Lutheran at a figure the board thought fair, and board members spent hours over several months dreaming about possible uses for the property. Proposals ranged from renovating the apartments and renting them at below-market rates to low-income families, to simply razing the dilapidated structure to get rid of the eyesore. Now, readers might think, given all the board's conversation and the emphasis of this chapter, that the board did a great job of gathering information from a wide range of sources and allowing this information to move freely throughout the congregational system and the neighborhood. We board members certainly thought we were providing good leadership and were excited about the many creative uses we had identified for the property.

Before long, however, we found out that we did not have nearly as much information as we thought, nor had we really explored our options. Our comeuppance came at the congregational meeting called to vote on purchasing the property. After a brief presentation by the board chair, the first question asked by a member of the congregation was, "What are the property taxes?" Those of us on the board just stared at one another. We had no idea. And the answer was important, because as long as the property's use was not directly related to the congregation's ministry, taxes could easily amount to four or five thousand dollars a year, a significant sum for Grace. The meeting went downhill from there, as members' skepticism rose, and understandably the congregation did not approve the purchase. Instead, members instructed the board to gather more information and solicit input from members and other interested parties.

Board members researched the cost of renovating the apartments, studied the tax implications of various uses, and talked with members and friends of the congregation. Among the needs identified were several related to accessibility. The church did have a parking lot, and of course, off-street parking is a great asset for a landlocked city church. But the lot was across a busy street made even more dangerous by an awkward jog in the equally busy cross-street. In addition, no matter which of the church's six entrances people approached, they had to deal with stairs. Folks had noticed that a few members and visitors found the barriers challenging enough that they did not return.

As the board discussed the options, this irony surfaced: Grace Lutheran Church had been founded to serve people who at the time constituted a minority group (among Lutherans) and did not feel welcome elsewhere. Community outreach was in the congregation's DNA. Further, Grace had been faithful to that identity, continuously welcoming neighbors, guests, and those in need of the social services offered in the building. But the parking situation and the design of the building itself kept people out.

Once the congregation acted with intelligence, the way forward became clear. The congregation voted to purchase the property, raze the dilapidated duplex, develop a small parking lot with four spaces reserved for the handicapped, and best of all, build a new entrance with an elevator. After decades of reaching out to people, the congregation became physically accessible to them. Worshipers who would have been forced to go elsewhere can now easily reach and enter the building, so now during worship, wheelchairs and walkers are parked in the aisles or in spaces created by shortening several pews.

The neighborhood ministries coordinator's position has been increased from half-time to full-time, and services have proliferated. A "diaper depot" provides diapers at low cost to qualifying families, and an after-school jobs program gives middle-school children something constructive to do for a couple of hours a week and teaches them responsibility and good work habits. Members staff a clothes closet and tutoring for students from area elementary schools. A free legal clinic is offered one Saturday a month, as is a free community meal prepared by members and open to anyone who wants to drop by.

## Information and Hope

After their false start, leaders and members of Grace Lutheran exercised intelligence—noticing and responding to information available within the congregation and its environment. At members' insistence, the leaders enhanced the congregation's intelligence by removing blocks to the free flow of that information and inviting greater participation in its exploration. In the end the congregation made a decision consistent with its identity through the decades as a congregation that reaches out to people overlooked by other groups. Leaders' and members' attentiveness to the information available and openness to the possibilities enabled the congregation to act in a way that has strengthened its ministry and reinforced its understanding of the mission it is called to carry out.

This story illustrates several key principles about how information functions in a flexible, resilient system:

- Systems are nourished by free-flowing, meaningful information— information that may be "startling, uncomfortable, even shocking."[40]
- Groups and organizations need a clear sense of purpose—"what they are trying to accomplish and how they want to behave together."[41]
- Organizations collectively use their purpose to interpret information—to determine what their work is and how to do it.[42]
- Ultimately, systems use new information to reinforce themselves—to become more who they really are.

Even when congregations intend to remain open to new information, we may feel threatened by these descriptions of the way our world works. Leaders and members do not usually want to hear that the average age of the congregation's members is rising, the state high-way department is taking a third of the church's property to widen a roadway, the denomination is publishing a new worship book, the community's school is consolidating with one in a town twenty miles away, a major discount retailer is building a distribution center across the road, a local manufacturing plant is closing—the list of possibilities is endless. But when we treat information as a source of nourishment, we can approach with curiosity the new thing God is doing in our community. Leaders and members together can exercise their collective intelligence to deal with the complexity of our world and the mission and ministries to which we are called in that changed situation.

# 2

## *Complexity*

## *An End to Childish Ways*

*M*ANY AMERICANS YEARN FOR A SIMPLER WAY OF LIFE. BILL wrote this chapter in Maine, where he has vacationed for thirty-seven years. Over those years, and especially in the past decade, he has met many people who left their higher paying but high-pressure jobs and frantic lifestyles to move to Maine for a simpler life. Most of us can sympathize with the move these people have made even if we are not ready to follow them. We frequently complain about the complexity of our lives.

On the other hand, we also understand the excitement of a person who makes a conscious decision to make her or his life more complex. A friend of Bill's recently accepted a position with a new company that is much more complex than her former job. She has moved from a small company in one location to a large company with five or six locations. She now has primary oversight for the most profitable division of this corporation, has many more employees under her, and reports directly to the CEO. Clearly, she has moved from a less to a more complex position. But in conversation, Bill has learned that she has not yet found her new employment more complicated. The former employer presented many complications because its financial position was not secure, its primary product was encountering declining sales, and both the employees and the shareholders were restless and lacked confidence in the direction the company was going. In other words, her former job pulled her in many directions at once—so she felt many pressures, from surly bosses to employees suspicious that they would be fired. So, we ask this question: is our issue with the complexity or the complicatedness of our lives? One of our scientist consultants addressed this question:

> Complexity as a concept sometimes has a bad connotation. Often people say that their lives are too complex, and they wish to simplify them. However, this is a confusion of scientific and colloquial terminology. They probably mean that they want some focus and convergence in their lives, so that they feel "together" and effective. In the scientific sense of the word, they actually want their lives to be *more* complex and less scattered. If their lives were truly "simple" (in the scientific sense of that word), they would follow repetitious rules every day. Complexity, by contrast, is related to the ability to create.

Life is incontrovertibly complex. This *complexity* is a given, one of the ways the world works, but systems can be more or less *complicated* based on many internal and external factors. Of course, not all interlinked and interactive systems are complex. Carol Albright uses the metaphor of the spider web and the fishnet to delineate complex systems. A fishnet has many connections but no focus or central point. A spider web also has many connections, but they are convergent. The spider web illustrates the nature of a complex system; a fishnet does not. Only from a convergent system do we get emergence—such as water from hydrogen and oxygen.[1] At the human level, most of us long for less complicated lives, but we are actually willing to make our lives more complex, especially if our lives are also thereby less scattered.

Complexity theory is rooted in concepts of self-organization and emergence through complexification. In the introduction and first chapter, we described the basic meaning of these concepts. *Self-organization* means that natural systems have a tendency to become more intricately organized all by themselves. As a result, new, unforeseen phenomena occur—a process called *emergence*. One example, we said, is water, which is very different from its elements, hydrogen and oxygen. In this example we also see that the whole is greater than the sum of its parts.

# The Scientific Theory

In this section we draw heavily from a book by Carol Rausch Albright, *Growing in the Image of God*, because it describes the basic elements of complexity theory in a very straightforward manner and summarizes well our wider reading in this area. We twice interviewed Carol, an accomplished author who writes in the area of neuroscience and theology, and her husband, John, a physicist, and discussed further questions through e-mail. In her book Albright cautions that complexity theories are relatively new and that not all scholars agree about them. However, she continues, scholars in a variety of disciplines refer to them, with increasing frequency, as a more or less settled assumption.[2] We will keep the tentativeness of these assertions in mind.

According to Albright, how the world became so well organized is not clearly understood, while disorder and disorganization have had strong theories connected with them for 150 years. A basic principle of disorganization is the second law of thermodynamics, which states that in a closed system there will be an inevitable increase in entropy (disorganization). The universe, by definition, is a closed system (no matter or energy can enter or leave), and therefore the universe is in a gradual slide (it is "running down") to nothingness. It is a "rather gloomy theory."[3]

While the closed universe is naturally running to disorder, almost all of life is an open system, in which matter and energy can enter or leave, and the effects of disorganization are countered. The earth, for example, is an open system receiving energy daily from the sun and radiating energy into space. Humans are open systems that "import" food, water, and air and dispose of carbon dioxide, heat, and bodily wastes. Self-organization seems to counteract the disintegrative forces of entropy (although this theory exists within the larger framework of the second law of thermodynamics). With complexity theory, the mood seems more hopeful.[4]

While a single definition of *complexity* is difficult to find, Albright uses the term to "denote the presence of a web of interlinked and active connections: the more intricate the web, the more complex the entity."[5]

We have already seen that complex does not mean complicated. Complexification, however, can occur when there are "link-ups in patterns so that they become increasingly meaningful and productive."[6] An example is a network of colleagues who interact meaningfully among themselves to accomplish things that none of them could do alone. One group of people to whom this phenomenon applies would be our forebears, who founded a form of democratic government that had never before been seen and that has lasted almost 250 years so far.[7]

In nature things often become more complex on their own by becoming linked into increasingly complex entities known as self-organizing systems.

> In fact, entities in nature, left to their own devices, will join together. Atoms form molecules, which form compounds, which recombine to form more complex compounds, until they stand on the threshold of life. . . . Not everything that exists will complexify; much will remain simple. There are still many more bacteria than mammals. But over eons of time, increasingly complex and intelligent forms of life have appeared.[8]

Says Albright, complexification also occurs in sentient life forms. Social networks, and even economic systems, tend to complexify, drawing in more resources and players in patterns of increasingly complex interaction.[9]

A hallmark of complexification is that this process creates phenomena that are new and could not be predicted by observing their predecessors (emergence). In turn, if the results of emergence work, the new substance will again complexify and produce more emergents. Furthermore, complexification seems organized. Says physicist Paul Davies, "This organization was not built into the universe at its origin. It has emerged from primeval chaos in a sequence of self-organizing processes that have progressively enriched and complexified the evolving universe in a more or less unidirectional manner."[10] Finally, if evolution is the underriding principle of all biology, it also is a process by which life becomes increasingly complex.

Evolution is a prime example of emergence, a process that occurs at the level of reproduction. Successful emergent entities encounter challenges from their environments. Those that are able to adapt to changing and challenging conditions are most likely to survive and procreate. "Successful systems are always adapting, and they have both the freedom and the reliable resources that allow them to adapt. That is why these systems have come to be called complex adaptive systems."[11]

Thus, "complexity develops best where there is not only freedom but also order. Complex adaptive systems at all levels are found most robustly on the cusp between order and openness . . . [and] are not found at an extreme of either order or disorder."[12] Life thrives where there is some order and some disorder: lawfulness and openness, predictability and contingency, dependability and freedom. This theory acknowledges trial and error, contingency and chance. Order is not all good and chaos is not all bad. "It [complexity theory] also denies the final validity of linear thinking in which developments must follow a logical progression. This new version of 'the way things really are' expects unpredictable emergent events and entities, networks, feedback loops and dynamic developments."[13]

Our human bodies and our brains are themselves complex adaptive systems. Our bodies maintain homeostasis by continually adapting and changing. Our bodies are never quite at rest. Our brain is the most complex natural system in the universe. "To date, the long process of complexification in the evolution of the universe seems to have peaked right here."[14] The brain is an example of the entire process of complexification in miniature, including the unique connections between brain (cells) and mind (what you are experiencing, consciously or unconsciously, all the time)—and how they relate and adapt to one another. Albright understands the mind and brain, while distinct, to have an inevitable basic commonality, as do mind and body.

Because relating and adapting to one another are critical for life, we now understand processes are as important as "things." This point of view goes contrary to the common assumption that things are somehow more "real" than processes. As we observed in our introduction, we see this mentality sometimes among church boards, which automatically think it more important to buy nearby available property for more parking (a thing) rather than to use the resources to develop a dynamic youth ministry. We have said that processes are

crucial in complex systems, and processes often depend on relationships. Consequently, relationships become just as vital as processes.
"Our personal networks become ever more complex because electronic
communications allows for the construction of more links than ever
before among individuals and organizations. These links are active in
nature: *they only assume reality through their relational process.*"[15]

## *Scripture*

As we develop implications of complexity theory for leadership in
congregations, we also build on the apostle Paul's well-known com-
mentary in 1 Corinthians 13:11: "When I was a child, I spoke like a
child, I thought like a child, I reasoned like a child; when I became an
adult, I put an end to childish ways." That is, social scientists' insights
around constructive developmental theories and psychosocial theories
inform human complexity theory.

Psychosocial theories go back to the work of Sigmund Freud, who
described psychosexual development; Erik Erikson, who developed
an eight-stage theory of psychosocial development; and Abraham
Maslow, who formulated a hierarchy of needs that people work to
satisfy. Psychosocial theories were popularized by researchers such
as Daniel Levinson and associates in *Seasons of a Man's Life*; Gail
Sheehy in *Passages*; and others. Constructive-developmental theories
focus on cognitive processes by which knowing is achieved. Of special
note is Jean Piaget's four-part stage theory of cognitive development
and Lawrence Kohlberg's thirty-year study of moral development. In
the religious front, the person who incorporated both psychosocial
insights and constructive-developmental processes into his theology
was James Fowler, especially in his book *Stages of Faith*. These developmental theories are examples of increasing complexity.[16]

A second scripture section that helps us reflect on complexity
within congregations is the book of Acts, Paul's letters, and the Pastoral
Epistles—1 and 2 Timothy and Titus. An inevitable metamorphosis
took place as the Christian community developed from a movement
toward an institution. During Jesus's earthly ministry, his followers
were a movement with little, but already some, organization. Note
that three disciples (Peter, James, and John) were chosen for special

responsibility, and that certain women accompanied Jesus and provided for Jesus and the Twelve out of their resources (Luke 8:1-3).

In Acts this incipient movement was called the Way, and already it had a little more organization (note, for example, the way Judas Iscariot's position was filled). By the time of Paul's journeys and especially because of his ministry to Gentiles, we see yet more structure as Paul received instructions from the "leaders in Jerusalem." Although this is not the place for a detailed analysis of these texts, note especially the Council of Jerusalem in Acts 15 and Paul's collection of funds for Jerusalem (Acts 11:27-29; Rom. 15:22-29; 1 Cor. 16:1-4; 2 Cor. 8-9; Gal. 2). What we see in the Council of Jerusalem is a more complex organization in which Paul had to seek "permission" of the leaders of the early church to be able to continue his ministry to the Gentiles. Jerusalem was "headquarters" for this burgeoning movement. Moreover, Paul's passion for money for the poor in the Jerusalem church had as much to do with Paul's thinking organizationally that the church must be one—not split between Jews and Gentiles—as it did with the need for the actual money for the poor.

Moreover, by the time of the Pastoral Epistles (which are among the latest writings in the New Testament), we see an even more formal and complex organization of the church. There are rules for proper decorum in life and in church (1 Tim. 2:1-15), qualifications for the office of bishop and deacons (3:1-13), instructions for teaching and preaching in the church and warnings against false teachers (4:1-5:24), and instructions for those who are slaves (6:1-10). So, inevitably we see in these passages evidence that the growth of the church meant the church was becoming more organized and complex, as new offices and positions in the church were emerging. Increasing complexity through self-organization and emergence in the individual congregations and in the whole organization of religious institutions occurred throughout Christian history and continues today. One way to examine this phenomenon is to explore what happens in congregations.

## Complexity and Congregations

Steve Doughty, a Presbyterian minister and author who leads spiritual retreats, reports that an increasing number of attendees of his spiritual retreats describe themselves as "church alumni," those who used to attend church faithfully but no longer do so. Doughty suggests that it is apt to describe these people in a phrase from John Milton of four hundred years ago: "The hungry Sheep look up, and are not fed."[17] Most of us regular churchgoers have an increasingly large group of church friends whose children grew up, moved to new locations, and have not found congregations that address their spiritual needs. There seems to be a paucity of congregations that understand the complexity of our world. As Margaret Wheatley puts it, "We want our organizations [read "churches"] to be adaptive, flexible, self-renewing, resilient, learning, intelligent—attributes that are found only in living [open] systems."[18] Instead, these seekers find congregations that are largely closed into a comfortable way of serving those who are still active there. These closed churches are organized, but they are not focused on what they are supposed to be about, and passion for mission is largely absent. As a result, many of these children give up on being part of a congregation and become another group of "church alumni."

We know that living systems must be open to change and that static living systems die. We know that openness to the environment over time spawns a stronger system, which of course means that open systems must be in a state of nonequilibrium, so they can change and grow. Therefore, congregations that understand themselves to be open systems, capable of self-renewal through change, flourish. These congregations understand that equilibrium is a false goal and that there must be a level of disequilibrium to avoid deterioration. Of course, most congregations, as Wheatley points out, equate a desire for equilibrium with a false definition of simplicity, which is what some people think they want. Equilibrium is a false goal. Some children and indeed people of all ages seek disequilibrium, novelty, lack of control, surprise. They live out a basic insight about the way the world works: one cannot have order without disorder.[19]

How can we learn to trust disequilibrium? We can trust that God is creating the world in such a way that living systems tend to self-organize, a phenomenon we introduced in chapter 1. "All living systems have the capacity to *self-organize*, to sustain themselves and move toward greater complexity and order as needed."[20] Evidence of self-organization surrounds us in our daily lives. Teachers in public schools, colleges, and seminaries now lead some of their classes in such a way as to give students a chance to self-organize. In his classes, Bill sometimes breaks the whole class into smaller discussion groups. He gives the students three or four reflection questions, sets a time limit, and asks them to pick one of the questions and address it in any manner they choose, so long as they have a report to give the whole class when the time period is up. Notice that these students need to organize themselves: Who will be their leader, reporter, and scribe? Which of the questions will they choose? In what medium and manner will feedback be given to the entire class? Will there be a majority and minority report? Will they decide by consensus or by majority? The issues of organization to be decided in a brief time are complex, yet almost every group succeeds in this task. However, the groups have very different ways of getting to the end point, and one can never predict what process any group will use.

Because we can trust that self-organization occurs, leaders, including pastors, can ease up on the need to control, which often holds back the creative energies of parishioners. When people understand the purpose and real values of their church (recall the image of a spider web's focus), their individual work will move toward system-wide coherence, or identity, the first ingredient required for a system to self-organize—a topic we also discussed in chapter 1. Pastors and leaders work to build meaningful relationships in order to establish connections and spark others' imagination rather than control. "When leaders strive for equilibrium and stability by imposing control, constricting people's freedom and inhibiting local change, they only create the conditions that threaten the organization's survival."[21] Systems can do themselves what leaders sometimes think they have to impose.

## A Clear Sense of Identity

A clear sense of identity and purpose is the essential foundation in a congregation open to outside influence, one that is able to self-organize and is willing to change, knowing that any change will be consistent with who (and whose) it already is. Also, we know that commitment and loyalty to the stated purpose of the congregation is essential for the well-being of the congregation. However, we also realize that establishing this strong, articulated sense of identity is not easy, especially in established congregations. Earlier we learned from science that organisms and organizations thrive best when some things are stable (identity) and some things are in flux. We learned that when a system has too much order, it dies. On the other hand, if it has no firm identity, it disintegrates into chaos and also dies.

## The Importance of Information

While a strong sense of identity is the first ingredient for a congregation to be able to self-organize, the second ingredient is *information*, especially new and disturbing information.[22] As we discussed in chapter 1, information is the nutrient of self-organization and becomes the medium of the organization.[23] A congregation that understands the essential place of new information amplifies new and disturbing information (for example, beginning changes in the demographics of a neighborhood) and is able to change, in a manner consistent with its core identity, to meet the new situation. In most congregations, new disturbing information is buried. In contrast, self-organizing congregations have a great capacity to adapt as needed.

In congregations usually only the acknowledged leaders' apprehension of new information is deemed worth listening to. But it is often those congregants at the margins who have a better handle on new information necessary for the church. For example, the people at the margins may not be more active because they are not being nourished spiritually by the congregation and have valuable suggestions about what ought to change to reach people like themselves. Also, these people at the margins often have closer relationships with totally unchurched people. Or the people at the margins may be those of a different ethnic or economic group who are just beginning to move into the community and are invisible to most of the active members.

The point is that, because of the multiplicity of sources for new knowledge, information in a congregation is most helpful when every person's voice is heard. Whenever any congregant or even an outsider brings new (perhaps disturbing) information, such news needs to be shared with everyone, because different people see different things and may propose ways of addressing the issue that others would not have considered. Wheatley observes, "There is a need for many more eyes and ears, for many more members of the organization to 'in-form' the available data so that effective self-organization can occur. But it is information—unplanned, uncontrolled, abundant, superfluous—that creates the conditions for the emergence of fast, well-integrated, effective responses."[24]

## Relationships

The importance of open information shared by everyone points to a third key ingredient for self-organizing churches—*relationships.* "Through relationships, information is created and transformed, the organization's identity expands to include more stakeholders, and the enterprise becomes wiser."[25] Although we introduced relationships in chapter 1 and will discuss them further in chapter 3, for now we point to a primary learning from life: nothing lives alone. Interdependency and connectedness are the pathways for life to flourish. In fact, scientists speak of the interrelatedness of all life. The lesson for us as leaders of congregations is that we ought to be forming dense webs of connections with one another and the communities in which we are embedded.

In a telephone conversation, Wheatley affirmed that relationships are more foundational than a new worldview of leadership. Yet we must understand her comment in context. Relationships form the core from which congregants will consider a new worldview of leadership, a worldview that is based on collaboration and cooperation rather than a hierarchical, top-down approach. A network of relationships comes first. Even in terms of relationships, we will see in chapter 5 that family systems theory suggests ways that leadership based on relationships may be enhanced or thwarted.

Our main point is that Wheatley fully understands the importance of a new paradigm. As Albert Einstein noted many years ago about worldview, "The kind of thinking that will solve the world's problems will be of a different order to the kind of thinking that created those problems in the first place."[26] In other words, when an objective seems impossible to achieve within the worldview that caused the issue, it may be reasonably easily accomplished with a new worldview.

However, Wheatley's concern is that readers think they understand the new paradigm and apply it in a very superficial way, and when it does not work, they think the worldview is not valid. Says Wheatley, "So I guess the caution is, 'Don't think you understand the paradigm too quickly.'"[27]

Wheatley gives the example of leaders who try, for example, to encourage widespread participation in the decision-making process and quickly run into all sorts of problems and conclude, "Well, that didn't work." "The next step is a common dynamic, which is to retreat back. The minute this new step doesn't seem to be working, we retreat back to the old approach, which is already not working."[28] She suggests that people have to remain curious, open, and humble, realizing that this is a profoundly different way of viewing the world—based on collaboration, relationships, love, and generosity. The best way we can prepare for the unknown is to focus on the quality of our relationships and recognize that everyone's information is important.

Of course, within congregations the role of information and the importance of relationships for developing more open, vital systems means we need to share at a more profound level than what we think about the coffee or who will win the football game this afternoon. It means focusing on God's will for the congregation. It presumes that, within the congregation, people can communicate well and relate profoundly about the deepest issues of life and the purpose of the church, so convergence of desired action begins to take place. And as convergence occurs, new levels of understanding emerge. For example, a congregation that had been dominated by the pastor and a few long-established members will become over time a network of relationships in which the needs of the community are recognized in a new way, and a new way of responding is designed. Just as important, a new process is being developed that will point to a new direction for interacting with the communities outside the church in the future.

## *Leadership in the New Paradigm*

We know scientifically that "our universe cannot be broken down into a few simple elementary units of matter. Not only is that ultimate simplicity based on false assumptions, but it undermines the very creativity of life which requires *complexity* as an essential dimension of all living systems."[29] This is the way the world works. Because the congregation is a complex system, this theory says that it is impossible to find simple causes to explain significant problems, that quick fixes are an oxymoron, and that we ought no longer try to blame one person for problems. Identifying a scapegoat bears little fruit. Meaningful change takes years. Many consultants suggest that significant, lasting change averages five to seven years to accomplish.

A congregational consultant described the futility of the old way of trying to correct problems in the church. He was taught that he could analyze congregations, deal with the problem areas, make suggestions that would work—and the problem would be fixed. He has learned that this approach rarely works. That is, the claim that simple solutions can be found for complex issues is a misconception. Change is situational and time consuming, and it requires a web of relationships with strong interconnections.

How do pastors lead within this web of influence rather than through a chain of command? One of our consultants told us that she loves the title of Ron Heifetz's book *Leadership Without Easy Answers* because it is so accurate to life.[30] With complexity, easy answers do not exist. Wheatley expresses what a leader who understands complexity offers:

> Leaders who live in the new story help us understand ourselves differently by the way they lead. They trust our humanness; they welcome the surprises we bring to them; they are curious about our differences; they delight in our inventiveness; they nurture us; they connect us. They trust that we can create wisely and well, that we seek the best interests of our organization and our community, [and] that we want to bring more good into the world.[31]

One of our consultants said that leaders in a web have to learn when to stand forward, stand beside, and stand behind. For most leaders, the most difficult of these leadership stances is standing behind. Because we are suggesting an approach to leadership that involves a change of worldview, more change is required of the pastor—as the spiritual, theological, and practical leader of the congregation—than anyone else. Many times the prospect of the personal change that is required discourages a pastor from leading at all.

Often leaders are pressured to come in and be a savior in a difficult situation. For example, many pastors are sent to congregations and told to "grow this congregation" or "clean up the mess in this church." This is a trap for pastors, because meaningful change comes, as we have seen, through a web of influence rather than autocratic command. "Organizations and societies are so complex, filled with so many intertwining and diverging interests, personalities, and issues, that nobody can confidently represent anybody else's point of view,"[32] says Wheatley.

Someone might argue in theory that in Christ, pastors and leaders can certainly represent one another's point of view. But in reality the preposition God uses in relationship to us is *with*. Immanuel means God *with* us. God does not take us over so that we cease to be individuals. *With* is the language of love, just as in a marriage one partner does not take over the other but stands *with* the other. Therefore, the faithful leader will understand her or his task is not to make each Christian a carbon copy of his or her neighbor, but to bring these people, with their divergent gifts and issues, into a meaningful relationship *with* one another and God. When pastors (or, occasionally, lay leaders) take on the savior role, they act as functional atheists—as if saying, "If I don't do it, it won't get done." In our paradigm, the pastor will help articulate what the church is about (identity), set a tone for what is acceptable given this identity, and help identify and cultivate leadership potential in people. The pastor will nourish curiosity instead of certainty. He or she will understand that all change is loss as well as gain and help others cope with the inevitable loss as the church, in its self-organization, is constantly in a process of change. The pastor will learn the truth of a quotation often attributed to Gandhi: "There go my people, I must hurry and catch up with them."

## Complexity and Size Transitions in Congregations

Twenty-five years ago, Episcopal priest and seminary professor Arlin Rothauge penned a slim but highly influential book, *Sizing Up a Con-*

*gregation for New Member Ministry,* to describe the very different ways leaders ought to encourage evangelism in congregations of different sizes.[33] In the intervening years, his categories have become so widely used that most pastors and many congregational leaders can describe churches as family-, pastoral-, program-, corporate-, or megachurch-sized. (This last category has been added since Rothauge's work.) In the past decade or so, particular attention has been paid to size transitions—moving a church from one size category to another—and to further expanding Rothauge's categories.[34] Unfortunately, space limitations will not allow us to describe each of these categories. Instead, we will focus on the transition between the pastoral- and the program-size church. It is generally acknowledged that this transition is very difficult and also one of the most common transitions congregations and pastors face.

One reason this transition is so difficult is that it involves a move from a single-celled church to a multiple-celled church. That is, it represents a move toward greater complexity. Family-size and pastoral-size congregations are single-celled units. This means that the people as a whole group relate to the matriarch or patriarch (in the family church) or to the pastor (in the pastoral-size congregation). However, in the program-size church, the people begin to relate primarily within different groups. Some may relate primarily with the music program and sing in one of the choirs; some may relate primarily to the Sunday school and its fine adult opportunities; and so on. The list where primary relationships are formed can be almost limitless. In fact, wise pastors and leaders will encourage the formation of many small groups that support the purpose (identity) of the church, for these small groups are where innovation and emergence often occur.

Think how difficult the transition from single-cell organism to multiple-cell organization is for the pastor and people. In the pastoral-size church, everything that occurs revolves around the pastor, who functions like the hub of a wagon wheel. The pastor is always there—at every meeting, social gathering, and outreach ministry event. The pastor visits the hospitalized and the shut-ins and calls on prospective members. When the relationship between pastor and laity goes well, the people relate to the pastor with the same warmth and affection that a collie gives its owners. (Of course, when the relationship sours, the people may act more like angry pit bulls!) The people like the arrangement because the pastor carries the ministry for them. And many pastors flourish in this arrangement because they receive continual positive feedback from the parishioners. The pastor's need to be needed is nicely fulfilled. Many pastors have been trained that the proper role of the pastor is to function as the hub of all activity. Beth once talked with a pastor who, when challenged to step out of this central role, pleaded, "It's the only way I know to be a pastor." Alice Mann points out that in literature, film, and on television, congregations are often portrayed in this pastoral image, and visitors will recognize them as "real churches."[35] Such views are being challenged as program-size and megachurches rise up, but culturally, the image of the pastoral-size church still predominates.

When a congregation transitions, or tries to transition, into the program-size church, basic changes take place. The pastor can no longer be at every meeting and event and cannot conduct the ministry alone. Suddenly those in the hospital discover that while the pastor visits some of the time, on other days laypeople involved in the Stephen Ministry make the hospital calls, and shut-ins discover the same. With this change, a lot of events occur and meetings are held where the pastor is not present, and the laypeople are invited to pick up the ball and carry on and, in fact, to initiate ministry. When this size transition is made, a portion of the members complain and want to return to Egypt—to have the minister always present.

Moreover, the change may be just as hard for the pastor. Her role suddenly becomes more complex. Instead of "doing" the ministry herself, the pastor now spends time training others to do this ministry and consulting with those in charge of different segments of the ministry. Instead of receiving continual feedback for her wonderful ministry, she spends more time as an administrator, training others so that they, rather than the pastor, receive most of the positive strokes. Moreover, the strategic planning for the pastor and congregational leaders becomes more complex, because they are now envisioning multiple ways to extend their ministry, looking for human and physical resources to accomplish new ministries, and providing encouragement and support for the many people doing the ministry.

We have had several pastors come to us with a story something like this: "I have been pastor of St. John's for twelve years now. In that time we have grown in worship attendance from 120 people per Sunday to 240-plus per Sunday. This congregation has always functioned as a pastoral-sized church, and unfortunately, I have fulfilled their expectations. Now we have grown so large that I'm being run ragged. Can I transition this congregation into a program-sized church, or do I need to resign, so that a new pastor can come in and function as leader of the program-sized church from his inception?"

On the opposite side of the spectrum, we have also witnessed pastors who have been called to a program-sized church and who downsized the congregation as quickly as possible to a pastoral-sized one. Predecessor pastors led the congregation without being directly involved in many of its ministries. But the new pastors seem to need the affirmation that comes from being directly involved in all aspects of ministry, and they can conceive of no way of leading but by being in charge of every event. Studies have shown that people can manage only about 150 relationships at a personal level, so the pastoral style severely limits the size of that church. We say this even though we know of congregations of well over three hundred who function in the pastoral style. Of course, we are also looking at workaholic pastors (prime candidates for burnout) and congregations in which the beginning signs of stress in that system are noticeable.

From our vision of leadership incorporating the insights of complexity theory we have traced in this chapter, we make these suggestions not only for leaders of pastoral-sized churches, but for leaders in any size congregations. Pastors should move deliberately—although such change will not happen overnight—from a model in which they are the hub of the church to one in which, when they lead, they sometimes stand forward, sometimes stand beside, and sometimes stand behind the laity. As someone has said, "We [pastors] ought to fail people's expectations at a rate that they can stand." If parishioners expect that their pastor will carry out the church's mission on their behalf, then this presumption ought to be challenged in a loving manner. The church's mission will flourish best in a web of relationships, when pastors and members rely on one another to engender a vision for that church's ministry and work together to carry out that mission. In this process, the pastor may have to let some programs, events, classes, even ministries die until lay leaders who feel called to keep them going emerge.

Unfortunately, even a pastor who leads a program-sized congregation and understands that she cannot be involved in every aspect of the life of the congregation can still function as an autocratic leader. In other words, she can command that others do the ministry but only in the way that she delegates. This style of leadership is as antithetical to the insights of this book as is the pastor who needs to do the ministry for the congregation and always be in command. However, a pastor without the emotional need to be constantly in charge can best empower the laity for their ministries and lead in a way that helps a congregation function faithfully and healthfully by understanding and utilizing the complexity in the congregation. Such a leader will understand that the key to effective leadership is operating within a network of relationships where the pastor attends especially to the integrity and function of the entire web.

## Complexity and Moral-Spiritual Development in Leaders

Those of us who incorporate children's sermons as part of our regular worship service soon learn that when we say, "God is like . . ." we have gone beyond the mental capacity of the preschoolers.[36] Their minds have not yet developed to the point that they can understand simile. Pastors who know Piaget's four-part stage theory of cognitive development understand that as children mature, their ability to comprehend reality becomes more complex until they are able to handle abstract thinking.

Since Freud at least, we have come to understand that as humans mature, they also grow in their mental and moral abilities. As we indicated at the beginning of the chapter, constructive development theories associated with people such as Piaget and Kohlberg, and psychosocial theories associated with Freud, Erikson, and Maslow are widely known. Levinson and associates and Sheehy have popularized psychosocial theories.

James Fowler, a Christian practical theologian, has incorporated the work of these pioneers into the foundation of his theory of faith development. Fowler has identified six developmental stages in the way faith functions in people's lives. The six stages occur in an invariant sequence, and all people move through the same sequence of stages, although very few reach stage six. In fact, people may stop their faith development at any of the six stages. This development is partially and progressively conscious but is in large degree unconscious. Fowler's six stages are: (1) intuitive-projective faith (early childhood), (2) mythic-literal faith (school years), (3) synthetic-conventional faith (adolescence), (4) individuative-reflective faith (young adulthood), (5) conjunctive faith (midlife and beyond), and (6) universalizing faith.[37]

Elsewhere we have argued that mainline definitions of faith prohibit us from calling moral/spiritual developmental stages "stages of faith."[38] However, it would be foolish not to understand that, as humans grow and mature, understanding, appreciation, and questioning of religious viewpoints become more complex. In this regard, these developmental studies stand as a specific illustration of complexity theory. In religious circles, Fowler's work has been widely read, affirmed, critiqued, and used to understand how individual Christians and whole congregations view their relationship with God. Many Christian speakers and writers have built on Fowler's stages of faith or adapted them to language they find more helpful. Two such writers are the couple James D. Whitehead, a pastoral theologian, and Evelyn Eaton Whitehead, a developmental psychologist. Insights from an audiotape by the Whiteheads presenting a developmental vocational model offer further insights on complexity.[39]

From a Christian perspective, vocation is God's calling us to serve God and God's creation. Vocation always begins with God—God's choosing us as beloved children. That is, before God asks us to live a certain way, God claims us as God's own. At Gettysburg Seminary we have long called the priority of God's action over our response "because . . . therefore" language, as opposed to the usual "if . . . then" language of human organizations. Note the contrast: "If we earn good enough grades, then we will get into the college of our choice." "If we are good enough people, then God will reward us with everlasting life." However, gospel language is the opposite. "Because God has claimed us as God's own, therefore God calls us to live as God created/creates us to live." Baptism is God's affirmation of us and claim on us. Faithful Christians spend their lives in response, asking, "How do we live in/into our baptism for a lifetime?" The way we live is our vocation.

In other words, baptism is both completed at the font and a lifelong continuing event, as every day God washes our sin away and raises us as God's new creation. Our physical death is our final dying to sin, and our resurrection marks the completion of the baptismal event. So, in response to God's claiming us in baptism, vocation is a lifelong relationship with God, a lifelong conversation with God, with all the ups and downs that occur in a human relationship.

The Whiteheads suggest that the first way we live out our vocation is as a *child of God*. In this stage, ideally, we learn to trust God and others through the loving nurture of our parents and other caregivers. As children of God, secure in God's love of us, we learn to play. We learn that we can experiment and try things and change rules, and such changes are okay because they do not destroy the love bond. A virtue of this stage is that we learn flexibility. A group of older grade school or middle school boys and girls go to the park to play baseball, but there are not enough children to form two whole teams. So children change the rules: you can only hit to the left of second base (opposite for lefties); the batter runs to first base, but if the ball gets to the pitcher on the pitcher's mound before the batter reaches first base, the batter is out. There are rules, but they are flexible and are adjusted to meet the actual situation at hand.

Flexibility grows out of a basic ability to trust. Centuries ago Martin Luther taught us a basic lesson about trust. "Anything on which your heart relies and depends, I say, that is really your God."[40] In other words, all people trust in something—if it is not God, then it may be money, position, power, or intellect. Or, rather than trust in material things, we might trust our intellect or spirituality, focusing on our capacity instead of trusting in God's grace. Some people are never able to trust, and all of us struggle from time to time with the question of whether we live in a trustworthy creation.

The issue of trust means that no one ever "completes" this stage. No one completely trusts God and God's way with creation; no one except Jesus has ever totally entrusted his or her whole life to God. And so throughout our lives, we return to this stage to learn again and again that we are beloved children of God. This is why we need to hear the gospel on a regular basis.

As Paul suggests in 1 Corinthians 13:11, as children grow toward maturity, we enter a second stage—that of *disciple*. Usually this change is not a conscious decision but "emerges" naturally as cognitive capacity develops. Subconsciously, the youngster is in a real sense "self-organizing" himself or herself to understand his or her environment more fully. This stage is more complex than being a child, because it involves conceptualization, abstract thinking, the use of metaphor, the interpretation of parables, and so on. At its base it requires interpreting God's Word in such a way as to be a faithful disciple.

Now, a disciple is a learner and a follower. We know that from the word *disciple* we have the word *discipline*. Christians at this stage willingly undertake a discipline to help them grow as disciples. Often, disciples will enter an apprenticeship, where they learn from a more experienced, mature mentor. At this stage, they begin to understand that the source of transformation and change is outside of themselves—in God's grace, to be sure, but also because of self-organization and emergence. These budding learners are in the process of internalizing the changes that occur as we move from being a child of God to disciples. One of the things disciples are often trying to do is "put on Christ" by responding in a faithful way to Christ's life. As part of the disciple's response, he or she investigates, "Who is my neighbor?" This is the stage at which people are most likely to wear bracelets that say, "WWJD—What Would Jesus Do?" To grow as disciples we read, study, converse, pray, work in small groups, and listen to our mentors.

According to the Whiteheads, disciples face two particular temptations at this stage. The first is seriousness. Disciples, like converts, may take *everything* seriously and have no sense of humor. Such people can sometimes be hard to live with, as they may remind us just what we are doing wrong or tell us what we must believe, pray, or do in any given situation. Living in Christ with those who see themselves as the spiritual vigilante posse can wear everyone out.

The other temptation, say the Whiteheads, is to refuse invitations to lead and remain perpetual students. The problem is not with being a perpetual student. Just as we never outgrow the need to be a child of God, so we also never outgrow our need to be disciples. But the temptation is to become locked into this level of complexity rather than taking the further step from discipleship to leadership.

The final stage is what the Whiteheads call that of *stewards*. From the Bible (see especially Luke 12:35-48 and 16:1-13) and from the ancient Grecian world, we know that stewards were often slaves who ran a rich person's estate while he (in a paternalistic world, it was almost always "he") attended to politics or was away from the estate. Sometimes the steward was the estate owner's wife (remember the low status of women in that society), to whom the husband entrusted the care of his property while he was off involved in the highest goal for a person of his status—being involved in politics.[41] On the one hand, the steward owned no property or estate himself. He was caretaker of what belonged to another. On the other hand, the steward had great authority, being able to transact any business in the owner's name. He had the signet ring of the rich owner (a ring was often used in place of a signature in a preliterate society) and could enact transactions as if he were the owner.

In the parable of the dishonest steward (Luke 16:1-13), we see a steward transacting in place of the master but cheating the master, and hence eventually being called to account by the owner. Ideally, however, the steward was an authoritative administrator who ran his owner's estate efficiently and economically. Notice the complexity of living as stewards. The owner does not give day-to-day instructions on how to administer the estate, but rather entrusts to the steward the entire running of the estate.

Because a steward is one to whom other workers look for leadership, the Whiteheads use this term for the most complex way of living the Christian life in community. Such a change from disciple to steward (leader) again emerges naturally. That is, after many years of serving as good disciples, parishioners may look around and realize that they are among the experienced people at the church, that others are beginning to look to them for leadership, and that they have begun to provide it. Upon reflection, they realize that they are stepping into leadership positions and living as stewards without really having consciously noticed the change. Their leadership has emerged from their discipleship. They finally realize they are serving as authoritative servants, through an authority earned by respect. These disciples often begin living as stewards by serving with others in planning and executing ministries and later in creative visioning.

Again, the Whiteheads point to two temptations of the steward as authoritative servant. The first is possessiveness. "It's my program and I'm in charge." Whether an enterprise involves "my kids," "my committee," "my church," or "my idea," we are always tempted to become control freaks. This possessiveness means moving from servant leadership, acting in a network of relationships (where everyone's voice counts), to command-hierarchy leadership (where I make the decisions). As this person considers her leadership as her territory to control, she begins to use the possessive more and more. Of course, it is not my church, my project, or my plan; it is the Lord's (remember the steward owns nothing). To exercise leadership collegially means to work in a network that empowers all.

The second temptation is that of paternalism or maternalism—the "father knows best" or "mother knows best" syndrome. We do not have to be a parent or be of a certain age to fall into this temptation. We only have to care for people and have people or programs under our responsibility. This deep desire to care sometimes goes one step too far and becomes restraint. Furthermore, the Whiteheads suggest, when you put possessiveness ("It's mine") and paternalism ("I know best") together, you have a tyrant.

Increasing complexity occurs as people move naturally from one stage to the next, but the complexity is rooted in more than a new stage emerging from the last. In order to combat the temptations of any stage, all three ways of living—child of God, disciple, and steward—must simultaneously be held in balance. The greatest complexity that emerges is keeping these ways of living in dynamic tension with one another, like a juggler keeping three balls in the air at the same time. Attending to our child, disciple, and steward simultaneously is something we usually do subconsciously as we live the complex lives of mature Christians.

In this chapter we have seen that complexity and complexification are a part of the way the world works through evolution, and that complexification accompanies an individual's maturation biologically and as a Christian. We note that when people say they want to lead simpler lives, they really mean less complicated lives, not necessarily less complex lives. We have seen that congregations are complex organisms that live most faithfully when, out of a core identity, they are open and flexible, alert to new and disturbing information from any source. These churches demonstrate a willingness to be in a constant state of change that depends upon understanding themselves as complex and diverse. Congregations stuck in an identity that is not open to significant change usually do not see how complex they actually are. Of course, individuals and congregations do fight against meaningful change at times, but when such churches understand complexity, they are more likely to perceive a vision and to welcome change in order to live into that vision. A basic ingredient for such a vision with its complex ramifications is building and sustaining meaningful relationships.

# 3

## *Interrelatedness*

## *Reconciling the World*

SINCE 1999 SEVERE DROUGHT HAS AFFECTED LIFE THROUGHOUT THE western United States and beyond. Many reservoirs hold less water than they have since the 1950s. In some areas, water levels are the lowest they have been since the Dust Bowl era, while in the northern Rocky Mountains, water levels are the lowest ever recorded. Not all effects from the drought are visible, however. For example, aquifers—natural underground holding tanks—are being depleted. Scientists, government agencies, and economists have been monitoring the impact of the drought from many perspectives and agree: the devastation is widespread.

Beth and her husband travel several times each year to fish in the West, so she is particularly aware of ways the ongoing drought has affected streams and rivers that flow into the Mississippi, Colorado, Columbia, and other watersheds. Many entities depend on those rivers. Utility companies supply hydroelectric power for the nation's electrical grid. Farmers irrigate their fields to feed people around the world. Barge operators haul crops to market. Cities supply water to individuals and industries. Vacationers look forward all year to a week of summertime fishing and boating. All these individuals and organizations pour millions of dollars into river-based economies and compete for access to these precious resources as an array of government organizations struggles to balance and regulate competing needs and desires.

Rivers are more than an important resource for humans, however. They have a life of their own, and drought damages them. Rivers slowly fill with silt because water flows are not strong enough to scour the riverbeds. The oxygen level in the water drops because less air is stirred into the slow-moving water. The temperature of the water rises as still, shallow pools heat up. Fish and other water creatures become stressed and may die from lack of oxygen and water temperatures higher than their systems can tolerate. Plant and insect life in the rivers is diminished, which again affects the fish and other river dwellers. Eventually eagles, osprey, herons, pelicans, geese, ducks, mergansers, and other birds that depend on the rivers move elsewhere to find food. Stressed vegetation along the riverbanks becomes vulnerable to disease, predation by insects, and fire, which in turn affects wildlife. And so it goes. The intricate relationships among water and land, plant and animal life are almost too vast and complex to comprehend, even if we look only at portions of the drought scenario related to the West's rivers.

## The Theory

Throughout this book, we use science cautiously. For example, we do not make direct connections between the quantum world and human behavior. The premise of this book, however, is that certain principles observed by scientists are so widely held and appear to be so broadly applicable that we can say with a high level of certainty, "This is the way the world works."

The scientists with whom we met agreed: we see evidence throughout the universe that the interrelatedness of all things is a foundational principle. British priest and social psychologist Diarmuid O'Murchu writes that the conception of the universe as an interconnected web of relationships is one of the major themes that recur throughout modern physics.[1] Interrelatedness appears beyond the quantum world, however. An astrobiologist we spoke with noted that scientists used to try to describe how an individual star emerged; now they realize that stars emerge in clusters and greatly influence one another. Another scientist observed that all reality is made of the same basic material. That is, the ground, the earth, and the stars consist of the same matter. We all share the same genetic code; we all make very similar kinds of proteins; we all consist of the same kinds of building blocks. Brian Swimme, a mathematical cosmologist, even proposes, "Our natural genetic inheritance presents us with the possibility of forming deeply bonded relationships throughout all ten million species of life as well as throughout the nonliving components of the universe."[2] In our chapter on complexity, we likened a complex system to a spider web—a system with many connection points as well as a point of convergence. Interrelatedness is the capacity for mutual influence between and among the elements of a web. Substance and process work together as a complex system and connect with yet other systems. Interrelatedness says the world consists of not only complex webs, but webs of webs!

One of the most fascinating examples of interrelatedness is the human brain. We noted earlier that the brain is "a web of interlinked and active connections"[3] characteristic of complex systems. Even the brain's structure demonstrates that it depends on relationships. The brain is composed of about one hundred billion neurons—about the number of stars in our galaxy. Each neuron has on one end a long, hairlike extension called an axon, and on the other end, tentacle-like structures called dendrites—as many as one hundred thousand per neuron. An axon from one neuron links up with a dendrite from another at a junction called a synapse. Neurons form on average about a thousand—but as many as ten thousand—synaptic connections, and these connections are where the brain's activity occurs.[4] Educator and longtime student of neuroscience Bob Sitze observes: "The theoretical number of possible connections among all the neurons approaches 40 quadrillion. Given the sheer number of possible connections at different levels of synapse strength, it is difficult to think or speak about your brain without the matter getting complex or even unfathomable. The phrase 'fearfully and wonderfully made' comes to mind."[5] Carol Rausch Albright suggests, "The nature of our brain and the messages it generates must provide some clues to the nature of the world itself."[6]

One clue to "the nature of the world" worth noting is that the brain, as complex as it is, does not function apart from many other systems. To one degree or another, the three-and-a-half-pound body of nerve cells depends on all ten systems of the human body—including the skeletal, muscular, circulatory, respiratory, digestive, and endocrine systems. It requires internal input—electrical and chemical impulses that trigger the leap of signals from one neuron to another. It also requires external stimulation—movement and data we process as sights, sounds, feelings, and the like, and extended deprivation can result in extreme anxiety, hallucinations, bizarre thoughts, depression, and antisocial behavior.[7] Of course, the brain has a role (to say the least!) in each person's interactions with other people as well as the entire environment. So the brain is a complex system that consists of and interacts with other interrelated complex systems.

Like the brain, a river is one focal point for a web of structures and processes. Its many systems might be of interest to the geologist, hydrologist, ichthyologist, entomologist, botanist, economist, agronomist, farmer, urban planner, resort owner, sporting goods retailer, and many others. Of course, a brain and a river are only two of the many realms in which the interrelatedness of the universe can be seen, but both show us that the phenomenon is about webs of webs. Given how foundational interrelatedness is, we can say, "This is the way the world works." From microworlds to macroworlds and in the interplay among them, we see the principle in action.

## *The Witness of Scripture*

Scripture has much to say about the interrelatedness of life. So interconnected is creation, the tradition says, that humankind, along with every animal of the field and every bird of the air, was formed out of the dust, the ground (Gen. 2:7, 19; recall that *adam* comes from the Hebrew *adama*, "earth, dirt"). Psalm 8 attests to the interrelatedness of creation: the heavens ("the work of [God's] fingers"), human beings ("a little lower than God"), and "all sheep and oxen, . . . the birds of the air, and the fish of the sea" reveal God's majesty in all the earth. This unified creation both rejoices and suffers as one entity. We read in Psalm 148 that the heavens and its angels; moon and stars; the waters, mountains, and hills; fire, hail, snow, frost, and wind; fruit trees and cedars; sea monsters, wild animals, cattle, creeping things and flying birds; as well as all humanity—kings and princes, men and women, young and old, all together praise Yahweh. Yet Paul wrote to the Romans, "For the creation waits with eager longing for the revealing of the children of God. . . . We know that the whole creation has been groaning in labor pains until now" (Rom. 8:19, 22).

Scripture's portrayal of creation as interrelated goes beyond the poetic anthropomorphizing of rocks and locusts, however. Everything in all creation is brother or sister to everything else. Humans themselves are understood as kin to both one another and the nonhuman creation, and humans are given specific responsibility to care for all creation (Gen. 1:26-28). The Torah provides detailed guidance for this care. For example, Israel was commanded to observe a sabbath for the Lord every seventh year and a jubilee every fiftieth year. During those years, the people were to refrain from sowing, pruning, or harvesting, and to give the land a complete rest (Lev. 25:1-12). Some scholars believe the jubilee was never carried out but was an ideal intended to remind the people that they were merely stewards of the land, which belonged to God. Even if that assessment is correct, however, the concern in Leviticus for the land, which itself was part of God's gift to Israel (Gen. 17:8), speaks to the essential relationship between it and the people of Israel.

The laws of Israel also demonstrated the understanding that all people are interconnected and gave special attention to strangers, orphans, and widows (see Exod. 22:21-24 and elsewhere). The people of Israel were commanded to remember that they themselves were once aliens in Egypt and that they therefore had a special motivation and responsibility to care for—to be in relationship with—those whose connections with family and nation had been broken. So important were these relationships with strangers and the poor that the law spelled out specific ways to provide that care: do not harvest to the edges of the field, and leave the gleanings from the wheat and the fallen grapes (Lev. 19:9-10). Further, the prophets frequently took Israel to task when the people failed to practice such kindness and compassion toward one another and these downtrodden ones (for example, Zech. 7:8-10).

In his preaching and teaching, Jesus followed in the prophetic tradition, constantly connecting with those whom others considered unworthy of his attention—children and women; the lame, deaf, and blind; Gentiles and other despised people; and finally, as Jesus himself hung dying, the criminal (Luke 23:43). While Jesus served those in need, he himself had needs and depended on others for support. Luke tells us that as Jesus traveled about "proclaiming and bringing the good news of the kingdom of God," he was accompanied by the Twelve as well as some women "who had been cured of evil spirits and infirmities . . . who provided for them out of their resources" (Luke 8:1-3). Jesus was not a solo act; he was interrelated with others as one who both served and received service, enjoying relationships of mutuality even with people his culture considered "the least."

The principle of interrelatedness appears in Scripture's understanding of the church itself. The apostle Paul frequently reminded the young churches to whom he wrote that believers are all related as members of the body of Christ (Rom. 12:4-5; 1 Cor. 12:12-31; Eph. 4:14-16). "Individually," Paul taught the Christians in Rome, "we are members one of another" (Rom. 12:5). To the church in Corinth, Paul wrote, "If one members suffers, all suffer together with it; if one member is honored, all rejoice together with it" (1 Cor. 12:26). Each member needs the others, Paul admonished the Ephesian Christians, and "the whole body . . . as each part is working properly, promotes the body's growth in building itself up in love" (Eph. 4:16). Using an image even richer than that of the web, Paul makes plain that the interconnectedness of the church's members is central to understanding its purpose and function.

That the church's bodily-ness is more than an abstract ideal is seen in the collection for the relief of the Jerusalem church Paul writes about in 2 Corinthians 8 and 9. Here we see the church at its best in an inspiring expression of its unity in Christ. During a time of "a severe ordeal of affliction" in Jerusalem, Paul reports, the Macedonian Christians "gave according to their means, and even beyond their means, begging [Paul and Timothy] earnestly for the privilege of sharing in this ministry to the saints" (8:3-4). Paul urged the Corinthians to share with similar generosity to achieve "a fair balance between your present abundance and [the Jerusalem church's] need" (vv. 13-14). Their sharing, Paul assured his readers, would do more than bring relief to the Christians in Jerusalem. "You will be enriched in every way for your great generosity, which will produce thanksgiving to God through us. . . . Through the testing of this ministry you glorify God

...while they long for you and pray for you because of the surpassing grace of God that he has given you" (9:11, 13-14). The sharing among these communities of faith would give rise to even greater bounty, benefiting the whole body of Christ and even bringing glory to God, who had already provided "every blessing in abundance" (v. 8). Good things flowed to and from everyone involved in the collection, which grew out of God's creative love.

Finally, Scripture witnesses to the culmination of creation's interrelatedness, Christ himself, whose work is to overcome the powers of sin and death that divide creation. Paul wrote to the Colossians in a passage known as the "cosmic Christ hymn" the good news that everything or "all things" (*ta panta*) are reconciled through Christ:

> [Christ] is the image of the invisible God, the firstborn of all creation; for in him all things [*ta panta*] in heaven and on earth were created, things visible and invisible, whether thrones or dominions or rulers or powers—all things (*ta panta*) have been created through him and for him. He himself is before all things [*ta panta*], and in him all things [*ta panta*] hold together. He is the head of the body, the church; he is the beginning, the firstborn from the dead, so that he might come to have first place in everything. For in him all the fullness of God was pleased to dwell, and through him God was pleased to reconcile to himself all things [*ta panta*], whether on earth or in heaven, by making peace through the blood of his cross. (Col. 1:15-20)

God's work through Christ is not for the benefit of humanity alone, but for all things. Before the beginning of time, all things were created through and for Christ. And in the fullness of time, all things will be reconciled in him. Christ's work is cosmic in scope and significance. Lutheran pastor Elaine Siemsen reflects on the meaning of Christ's resurrection:

> As we follow God's plan from creation to incarnation to Christ's life, teaching, death, resurrection and ascension, we experience the interconnected dependence of all things. These connections aren't just convenient for life or comfort: they are the foundation

of salvation. . . . As resurrected people, we can work for justice for each other and for all that God has made. As we die to sin and rise to Christ, we work for the restoration of honor and justice to all things already blessed by God. As we claim life in Christ, we live that blessing with the fields and rocks, trees and stars. The Resurrection is for all things, *ta panta.*[8]

God's command that Adam and Eve "have dominion over . . . every living thing that moves upon the earth" (Gen. 1:28) does not set humanity *over* or *against* the rest of creation. Human beings are in no way separate from the other works of God's hands. Rather, humanity is placed *within* God's world and given special responsibility to care for all things. The purpose of Christ's work is to reconcile the world to Godself (2 Cor. 5:19), "to gather up all things in him, things in heaven and things on earth" (Eph. 1:10), to overcome everything that interferes with the essential relatedness of *all* creation.

## *Interrelatedness in Congregations*

When we reflect on the interrelatedness of our world, we examine more than a collection of parts. Whether we focus on individual congregation members, the congregation as a whole, or even the church universal in every place and time, we see that each entity is a focal point in a complex web of relationships connected to still other webs. That image informs our reflections on interrelatedness in congregations. In her years as an editor, Beth has talked with more than one would-be author eager to write about a "systems approach" to some aspect of congregational life. Too often, however, the proposed book has exhibited an incomplete understanding of systems, particularly interrelatedness. A congregation is not just a collection of smaller groups—a board plus a Sunday school plus a youth group plus a women's organization, choir, evangelism committee, and so forth. Nor can we understand congregational systems simply by examining them from a variety of perspectives—those of leaders, longtime members, occasional visitors, neighbors, community leaders, denominational officials, and the like. Rather, interrelatedness is about what happens between and among the parts, how the parts and relationships work together as a complex system, and how they connect with other systems.

A congregation is both made up of and connected with many complex webs of relationships. Webs within the congregation might include people related by blood or marriage; people with particular interests, such as choir or band members, teachers, and those who can be counted on to oversee a potluck supper, paint a classroom, or tend the flower beds; and members of the many teams that lead the congregation's worship: greeters, ushers, nursery attendants, acolytes, lectors, assisting ministers, and those who care for the altar, design and sew banners, and so on. Each individual is in turn connected with many other webs, some of which may not directly involve anyone else in the congregation: their family of origin, perhaps a nuclear family, colleagues and classmates, neighbors, those who share hobbies and interests—the list is nearly endless.

Finally, webs within a congregation and the congregation as a whole are likely connected with other webs that reach beyond the congregation: other churches in the neighborhood or community; other congregations of the same denomination or faith; communities that support specific ministries, such as Habitat for Humanity or an orphanage in India; various community development or justice-related efforts; and the like. One of our consultants suggested that the church in the world today is perfectly positioned to connect other webs. For example, in a local community, congregations may serve as a meeting ground for the police department, library, county services, the neighborhood-watch people, those organizing to fight poverty, and others. No other single institution in society has the capacity to build bridges with as many other groups as the church does—because congregations have members everywhere.

Congregations themselves can also join together to make an impact on society we could not make as solitary Christians or a single congregation. We see an example of the power of such webs in Lutheran Services in America (LSA), an alliance of more than three hundred health and human service organizations in thousands of communities across the United States and the Caribbean. The member organizations provide services ranging from health care to disaster response, from services for children and families to care for the elderly, from adoption to advocacy.[9] The network, supported by nearly seven and a half million Lutherans in almost seventeen thousand congregations, is so large that it directly serves one in fifty Americans. President George W. Bush once spoke at a reception for leaders of major social service organizations, attended by Jill Schumann, president and CEO of LSA. On his way into the reception hall, social services providers stood three and four people deep to greet Bush. As he walked the line, he stopped, reached into the third row to shake Jill's hand, called her by name, and said, "We'll have to have lunch someday." LSA is significant enough in U.S. society that Bush's aides had prepped him on who Jill was. This is an example of the power of interconnectedness. According to Wheatley, if we are to take advantage of the lessons we learn from the principle of interrelatedness, we need to view life and all systems within it as dense networks of interdependent relationships.[10] Obviously, a congregation itself is—and is also part of—such a "dense network."

Wheatley further observes that to strengthen the systems we are connected to, we need to "attend to the quality of our relationships, the level of trust for one another, and whether by our own actions . . . we are doing things to bring people together, or we are doing things— intentionally or unintentionally—that are driving people apart."[11] Psychologist Daniel Goleman, author of *Emotional Intelligence*, concurs:

> When it comes to technical skill and the core competencies that make a company competitive, the ability to outperform others depends on the *relationships* of the people involved. . . .
>
> If the people in an organization cannot work well together, if they lack the initiative, connection, and any of the other emotional competencies, the collective intelligence suffers as a result.[12]

Everyone in the webs that converge in a vital congregation must attend to the relationships. We need to notice *how* we get together and *what* we are expecting when we get together.[13] If we come together in a congregation for worship expecting to have only a personal experience followed by a social hour, the congregation will not be built up in the same way as if we gather expecting to be brothers and sisters in Christ. Leaders—formal and informal, paid and volunteer; members; visitors; neighbors; and other friends and constituents are all connected through the congregational web, and we can all influence a congregation for both good and ill. By paying attention to the way we relate to one another, we are more likely to weave a strong web and create life-giving connections with other webs.

Wheatley related, "I listened to a woman minister who said that for everything she did, she applied one criterion: 'Is what I'm about to do going to weave the web or break the web?'"[14] Just as the strength of a web lies in the quality of its connections, the potency of a web of webs lies in its interrelatedness with other webs. The congregational web will be most vital when everyone in the faith community strives to fulfill his or her role as a member of the whole body of Christ, not merely our own congregations but God's church in every time and place. The web will be strengthened further when we act on the assurance that God was in Christ reconciling not only the church but "the world" to Godself. Ultimately, this interrelatedness creates the opportunity and the power to change the world, and, as one of our consultants observed, love is "the most powerful expression of power." Because each of us belongs to many webs, and every web is connected to many other webs, when we strive to build up one another in Christ, we become channels throughout the world for the greatest power of all, the power of God's creative, reconciling love.

## Interrelatedness and the Christian's Vocations

The classical doctrine of vocation (from the Latin *vocare*, "calling") provides a sturdy framework to help Christians understand and live out their interrelatedness with other people and all of God's creation. The Protestant Reformers were especially helpful, because they understood vocation broadly. Rather than claiming that only an elite group had a vocation, they defined vocation as *a Christian's calling from God to service in the world*. Vocation is inherently relational—as the saying goes, "You can't be a Christian by yourself"—because our vocations always involve service to some person or other aspect of God's creation. We could say that the first vocation took place when

God put Adam "in the garden of Eden to till it and keep it" (Gen. 2:15). Now, and into eternity, we are surrounded by a great cloud of witnesses who strengthen us for "the race that is set before us" (Heb. 12:1), and in time, we will join that throng and serve with these saints in mutual love (13:1). Throughout Scripture, we witness people's attempts to understand what it means to be called by God to faith and to service.

Five centuries ago, Martin Luther radically reframed the concept of vocation, intending to address the disarray of the church of his day, particularly the monastic system and the notion that some people had a "higher calling" that offered opportunity to earn salvation through human merit. Luther reminded Christians that they are *all* "a chosen race, a royal priesthood, a holy nation, God's own people" (1 Pet. 2:9). Recalling the ideas we have discussed in the first two chapters of this book, we can see that Luther drew on Scripture to name the church's identity. He also reached out for information that had been forgotten by the church of his day—information that was *new* in his environment, which resulted in reshaping whole segments of society. Religion professor William Placher gives us a few clues about how significantly the world changed because of Luther's teachings: "When Luther began the Reformation, about 1520, between six and ten percent of the whole population of Germany were priests, monks, and nuns. . . . Only a generation later, in Protestant territories, their number had dropped by two-thirds; monasteries and convents were almost entirely closed, and the vast majority of the clergy had married. Social changes are rarely more dramatic."[15]

Luther did not write the last word on vocation, of course. Following Luther, John Calvin, working in the midst of political and economic turmoil that to an extent had been provoked (although neither intended nor foreseen) by Luther, attempted to deal with new issues of social mobility. As the Reformation spread, groups and individuals throughout Europe promoted their interpretations of the founders' principles. In the centuries since, philosophers, theologians, and social reformers such as John Wesley, Dietrich Bonhoeffer, Dorothy Sayers, Dorothy Day, Thomas Merton, and others have further explored vocation.

Above we defined vocation as the Christian's calling from God to service in the world. What does this mean? First, it is helpful to distinguish between the *call to faith*—the call to a relationship with God characterized by trust, openness, and joy—and the *calling to serve* our neighbors. Of course, faith and service are related, as James admonishes: "Faith by itself, if it has no works, is dead" (James 2:17). The call to faith can never be separated from our callings. God calls *all* Christians to serve their neighbor, so vocation is central to the Christian's life on earth. Our works of love are our response to God's work to reconcile all creation through Christ. In the concept of vocation, we see the interrelatedness of grace and works; faith and service; and God, self, neighbor, and all creation.

It is also helpful to recognize that all Christians have vocations in various interrelated arenas. Luther usually distinguished between the "spiritual government," or the church, and the "earthly government," which he divided into political and domestic economy. In Luther's day the domestic economy included both family and work, or occupation, because most economic activity took place in the family. Given the realities of our society—where occupation and family vie for our time, energy, and commitment, it makes sense to treat occupation and family as separate vocational arenas. But how are we to understand "occupation"? Bill Diehl, a Lutheran business executive and pioneer thinker regarding "lay ministry" or "ministry in daily life," says, "Occupation is whatever one primarily does with one's time at any given point in life. A paid job is an occupation. But so, too, is the unpaid job of homemaker and parent. Being a student is an occupation. . . . A person who is out of work has an occupation—that of seeking a job."[16] From the work of these and other thinkers, we can identify four interconnected vocational arenas, or webs of relationships: church, community, family, and occupation.

## The Purpose of Our Vocations

God calls us to various vocations in these four arenas because we (our vocations) are among the tools God uses to provide for the ongoing care of creation and the reconciliation of all creation to Godself. Luther sometimes referred to our vocations as God's "masks," God's external, tangible acts of self-revelation in the earthly realm. In our fallen state, we cannot meet God face-to-face and live, so God remains hidden. God's hiddenness is not about God, however, as if God were too shy to stand up in front of all creation or delighted in sneaking up on folks like some Halloween prankster. God's hiddenness is about our human frailties—the reason God placed Moses in a cleft between two rocks before passing by him (Exod. 33:12-23). Just as God safeguarded Moses, God protects us by donning masks before going to work among us. Until the resurrection, what we see is the mask, not God.[17]

Swedish Lutheran theologian Gustav Wingren further explains this central idea: "Natural occurrences such as storms and thunder, or sun, or rich harvests are also God's masks. . . . In co-operation in vocation, man becomes God's mask on earth wherever man acts. . . . In his toil he is a tool in God's hand, . . . so that God reveals himself to others through man's actions."[18] When we are faithful to God's call to love our neighbor through service on earth—as we carry out our vocations—we become God's masks. We become part of God's grand strategy to care for all creation—for the birds of the air and the lilies of the field, and for "the least" in God's world. We carry God's creative love to all the world.

Our vocations are at heart about relationships. Through them, we participate in interconnected webs—among them, the web of those called to faith; the webs of church, community, family, and occupation; the web of all people; the web, as we read in Psalm 8, of every phenomenon, structure, and creature in the universe. As long as we are in relationship with anyone, we are called to serve. We have vocations.

On the grandest scale, our vocations are connections in the complex web of God's creation, a web that converges in Christ. But for Luther, at the center of each of the four vocational arenas in which we serve is the neighbor, the one who has any need. That is, to discern our calling, we look to our neighbor. When we see a neighbor in need, there we find our vocation. We then raise the question asked of Jesus: who is my neighbor? Wingren says, "Vocation means that those who are closest at hand, family and fellow-workers, are given by God: it is one's neighbor whom one is to love."[19] Religion professor Douglas Schuurman adds, "Christian vocation includes all aspects of cultural and social life" and "always widens the circle to include strangers and enemies, and even non-human communities of being in its embrace."[20] Identifying the specific neighbor whom we are to serve might not be easy, but if we want to know to what vocations God is calling us, we need to pay attention to those who depend on us for care, others we encounter, and those whose needs burden us—whether human or nonhuman, animate or inanimate, wherever we might find them.

Of course, it can sometimes be difficult to see the web of relationships in a person's vocation. For example, in the county where Bill lives, a retired man fixes bicycles all year round for the underprivileged. This man spends every day, mostly by himself, repairing the bicycles. His vocation seems quite solitary. Still, some people find the broken or used bicycles and take them to his farm; others take the bicycles to those who need them. So he is in relationship with those who bring him bikes, those who distribute them, and, from a distance, those who enjoy riding the bikes, the products of his handiwork. From one perspective, he is the point of convergence of a whole web of people who deal in these used bicycles! Even the recluse who "lives off the land" in a rustic cabin on the edge of the Bob Marshall Wilderness in remote western Montana has a vocation, a relationship with creation and a responsibility to care for it.

God calls us to faith, and that relationship, centered in Christ, is the foundation of our identity as Christians. At the same time, we are given various vocations, and in those relationships, centered in our neighbors, we serve all creation, the very creation to which we were born and in which we were called to faith. We find the purpose of our vocations and the purpose of the entire life of faith in this dynamic swirl of relationships.

## Vocations and Gifts

Another key element in a theology of vocation is God's gifts to us. We all have gifts, which God grants us to use in the service of our neighbors. Paul points out that there are "varieties of gifts" (1 Cor. 12:4) and uses the image of the body of Christ to make the case that every member's gifts—whether the member is a hand or an eye (vv. 14-17)—are needed. Schuurman and others distinguish between two types of gifts: "'spiritual' gifts to be employed in the service of the community of faith" and "'natural' gifts intended 'for the benefit of the wider human community.'" We will not trace all the steps in Schuurman's reasoning, but he argues that the distinction between spiritual and natural gifts breaks down: "In light of the comprehensive character of God's kingdom and purposes, it is legitimate to extend the New Testament emphasis upon gifts and callings in the church into gifts and callings in the broader society."[21] Schuurman's guiding principle is simple: "All gifts are given by the Spirit and are to be used to express love of God and neighbor, whether inside or outside the church."[22] Although Schuurman does not use the language of inter-relatedness, he clearly recognizes that our world is composed of "dense networks" that preclude our setting aside certain gifts for the exclusive benefit of the church.

While our gifts are important clues to our vocations, focusing exclusively on them may lead us to overlook or even reject callings meant for us. Placher and many others who write about vocation cite critically acclaimed author and Presbyterian minister Frederick Buechner, who brings together these two ideas—our neighbor's needs and our gifts—in a frequently quoted passage: God calls you to "the kind of work (a) that you need most to do, and (b) that the world most needs to have done. . . . The place God calls you to is the place where your deep gladness and world's deep hunger meet."[23] Buechner's rule of thumb is often fitting, but we see many examples in the Bible of people who were not glad to do God's calling, who insisted they did not have the gifts to do what God asked. Moses resisted: "Who am I that I should go to Pharaoh, and bring the Israelites out of Egypt?" (Exod. 3:11). Isaiah demurred: "Woe is me! I am lost, for I am a man of unclean lips!" (Isa. 6:5). Jeremiah balked: "Ah, Lord GOD! Truly I do not know how to speak, for I am only a boy" (Jer. 1:6).

We have all heard people object when offered an opportunity to serve: "I don't have time." "I'm too old." "Others are far more qualified." "I could never deal with. . . ." If in the end, like Moses and the prophets, these people relent and make the time, take the risk, or follow an inner sense of obligation or duty to undertake a calling, they might discover they do possess all the resources (gifts) they need to exercise this calling. Much to their surprise, they might be well able to teach confirmation, move far from family and friends to build a school or health clinic in a developing nation, or patiently and tenderly care for an ailing relative. Not every vocation is rooted in our personal gladness or provides us the opportunity to exercise the gifts we already know we possess. Indeed, many callings that meet human needs, callings we undertake out of love, are in themselves hard or unpleasant. Further, some people, especially the poor and oppressed, have few opportunities to realize many of their gifts.

Even if our vocations are difficult or do not allow us to exercise our gifts, however, we can still serve God and our neighbor. We might find satisfaction only in the knowledge that we are doing something to benefit others—perhaps simply earning a living to provide for the care of loved ones, but such activity is no less our vocation than those we fulfill with deep gladness. The call to faith, our callings to serve, the needs of our neighbors, and the gifts we have been given to carry out our callings are interrelated, and if we put too much emphasis on one aspect of these webs while excluding others, we break the connections that together create the vital web of a faithful Christian's life.

## Discerning Vocations

In the interrelated webs of faith and vocation, the primary indicators of our vocations are our gifts and our neighbors' needs. Sometimes, particularly in the context of the givens and duties of our lives, our vocations are clear, requiring little reflection. In many cases, however, our vocations are less clear. The question at the heart of all discernment is this: is the action I am considering God-centered and neighbor-directed? Given that we do not *choose* our vocations but are *called* to them, the task of discernment is best framed as listening for God's calling, rather than making up our own minds about what to do with our lives. Of course, we do make many choices in every vocational arena—family, community, church, and occupation. But we do so in the confidence that God is acting in our lives and in our circumstances. As we meet our neighbors' needs, we contribute to "the common good" (1 Cor. 12:7), recognizing that God works in "all things . . . for good" (Rom. 8:28).

What is required to serve the common good is not absolute or fixed. Different situations and different times may require different forms of service. Although Schuurman's work on discernment is intended primarily for college students, his ideas are applicable to those considering their vocations throughout life. Building on Schuurman's suggestions, we offer the following clues to our callings.

- Contributing to the glory of God: We glorify God when we use our gifts to serve our neighbors, but we can also glorify God by creating art, caring for plants and animals, and tending our ecosystem.[24]
- Conformity to Bible and human law: Our vocations will be consistent with the witness of Scripture and human law. God is not going to call us to carry out some injustice or corruption.
- A still small voice: Many of us wish God would speak to us *at least* in a still small voice, if not in a loud, booming one! Not many people hear such a voice, however, although many of us find that a recurring hope or dream or an unexpected invitation or open door turns out to be meaningful.
- Opportunities and limits: Swiss theologian Karl Barth advised there is a "normal range" of vocations to which God usually calls people during their life cycles. He also points to our "place in history"—"our citizenship, the century we live in, our family history, the political structures that govern us, our economic class, the church community in which we find ourselves,"[25] and so forth. Together, our places in our life cycles and history present opportunities and limits, although the biblical example of Sarah reminds us that there are exceptions![26]
- What comes naturally: Some people think they are not carrying out a "vocation" because their activities do not have significant public impact (such as finding a cure for cancer) or require great personal sacrifice (such as selling all one's possessions and moving to Haiti). Most often, however, our vocation is right in front of us and requires only that we do "what comes naturally."[27]
- The fruits of our actions: Sometimes we step forward, not certain whether we are on the right path, and then pay attention to what happens. We should not too quickly abandon an enterprise that seems difficult, thinking the challenges are a sign that we have not found our calling. Our vocations will not always be easy, but good fruit will still result.

- Communal wisdom: The best guidance comes from those who know us well. We see communal discernment exercised formally when someone thinks she might have a call to be an ordained minister. If an individual says, "God is calling me to be a pastor," the wider church is asked to weigh in. In most vocational arenas, parents, friends, pastors, teachers, coaches, and others can represent the community for us and guide us.[28]

This last clue reminds us that although we undertake discernment of our vocations as individuals, we need not do it alone. Faith communities in particular, one of the webs to which we belong, can support people seeking to faithfully carry out their vocations both in the congregation and in the other webs of which they are a part. Preachers must proclaim the good news that our lives have purpose and meaning in God's mission: we are privileged to participate in God's reconciling work in the world. Nominating committees, ministry coordinators, and others in positions to invite members into service must pay particular attention to the gifts that members and constituents possess but that they are not currently using and, if necessary, create new service opportunities and ministries to call forth those gifts. To be faithful to their own vocation "to equip the saints for the work of ministry, for building up the body of Christ" (Eph. 4:12), congregations must be faithful to this foundational principle: all Christians are called to God-centered, neighbor-directed service in the world—not only in the church but throughout creation, God's web of webs.

## Vocations and Senior Adults

As congregations seek to carry out their responsibility to help members discern their vocations in the world, they may notice that people need more guidance at certain life stages. Schuurman became interested in guiding young adults as a result of his years of teaching religion in Christian colleges, and people in that age group certainly deserve and require assistance in their discernment. Another group that increasingly yearns for wisdom and insight is older adults, especially those nearing or just entering "retirement," however they might define that for themselves. Congregations with a significant number of members who are Baby Boomers probably have a vocation to serve that group—to help them discern which webs they are part of, which neighbors' needs burden them, and what gifts for service they have been given.

Traditional seniors programs, such as social gatherings and homebound ministries, will continue to be important in many congregations, although perhaps in new forms and most certainly for an older segment of the congregation. New models for older adult ministry must be created, however. First, particular effort should be given to developing strategies to help seniors explore the full range of their giftedness for service in all the arenas where we are called. Second, effort should be made to assist them in identifying their neighbors—in their family, church, and occupation (whatever they do with most of their time), of course, but also throughout God's creation. Third, seniors should be offered both theological insight and practical resources—including other members' expertise regarding taxes, financial management, health, nutrition, exercise, housing, and the like—for dealing with the many challenges involved in both the exercise of their vocations and the experience of aging. Finally, wise congregations will attend not only to strategies for supporting seniors but to ways the congregation can receive and honor the gifts of those same seniors. They might ask, for example, "What does it mean for us to have 'elders' or 'sages' in our midst?" Developing and implementing the programming to carry out these four tasks will not necessarily be easy. Significant time, talent, and effort will be required. But congregations must discern their own gifts and callings and then seek to be faithful to their own vocations to serve these neighbors.

These suggestions for congregations' work with older adults are examples of the ways congregations can enhance the capacity of all members to live out their interrelatedness with others. Ideally, congregations will recognize that members' vocations to serve in God's interrelated creation have implications for the entire congregation, not only seniors. Drawing on the understanding that our vocations are about life in all God's world, congregations will want to help nourish, identify, and equip people of every age for their vocations. Then teens and young adults preparing for college or entering the workforce, new parents making decisions about day care for their children, and middle-aged adults feeling disenchanted with their work life and wondering if they are making a difference in the world will have a framework for reflecting theologically on their roles and discerning next steps. Having already practiced discernment of their vocations throughout life, by the time people begin anticipating or moving deeper into retirement, they will be better able to cope with the challenges of aging and more likely to find meaning in the ups and downs of life.

Our hope is that before long, Christians and the congregations of which we are members will simply assume that God's callings to us never end. We will all recognize that we have gifts, the gifts we need to carry out the vocations God has in mind for us. We will not have to be reminded that all members of the body are needed and that "the senior cannot say, 'Because I am not a young person, I do not belong to the body'" (1 Cor. 12:15, adapted). We will all gratefully and eagerly claim our places as part of God's new creation, the outcome of God's reconciling work in the world and the reason for our vocations.

## Ta Panta *and Our Vocations*

Through our vocations, we see the power of God at work in the world. We see in the very fact that we attempt to carry out our vocations, however imperfectly, as well as in the many successes we and our neighbors in need enjoy, that God is caring for creation through a great web of webs. When we look at our vocations in light of God's love for us, we learn that God's callings have a purpose greater than granting us an arena in which we might experience deep gladness, and, yes, even greater than meeting the world's deep hunger. Whether we are leaders or followers, whether a relationship is long-standing or newly established, whether a group sorts church newsletters for mailing or an individual leads a work crew in Tanzania, the interrelatedness among individuals, groups, and all God's creation is of global, time-less significance. The relationships we form and honor through our vocations—the ways we participate in our world, however small or large they may be—are part of God's grand scheme of reconciliation.

The individual human may be the focal point of one complex web of relationships, but that web is inextricably connected with the many other webs of God's living and nonliving creation. Benedictine sister and social psychologist Joan Chittister recalls the work of a group of sixth-century Celtic monks who established what historians say was the first monastic settlement in Europe. They built five small, cone-shaped rock cells on Skellig Michael, a pyramid of rock that juts 714 feet above the Atlantic Ocean, and lived off fish, small native plants, and birds. Chittister continues:

> Most striking of all about Skellig Michael, perhaps, is that this bare chunk of a mountain in the middle of the sea is over nine miles off the coast of County Kerry in Southwest Ireland. To reach the mainland would take a day's sail, and then only when the water was calm enough to allow them to even attempt it. To reach the summit, the monks chiseled, by hand, more than 2,300 stone steps into the surface of the mountain. . . . Up there at the top . . . life was raw, cold and remote.

Still, the monks knew what was going on across the seas and told the rest of the world about it. For more than five hundred years, "the monks wrote most of the history of that part of the world. They wrote about earthquakes in Gaul, about small pox epidemics, about cures for disease, about the plunderings of the Vikings, and about one social struggle after another over hundreds of miles away." Intent on living in direct relationship with God and nature, they participated in their surroundings. Indeed, though physically remote, they stayed in relationship with their whole world, including far-off "neighbors."[29] So interrelated is God's creation, so vital are the ties that bind us, that even a people who sought to set themselves apart remained intimately connected with God's whole wide world.

Feminist theologian Elizabeth Johnson writes, "Woven into our lives is the very fire from the stars and the genes from the sea creatures, and everyone, utterly everyone, is kin in the radiant tapestry of being. This relationship is not external or extrinsic to who we are, but wells up as the defining truth from our deepest being."[30] Formed from the dust of the ground, all people are interrelated with the rest of God's dust-born world, just as every aspect of creation is connected with every other substance and process—and with us. The dense, interconnected networks that make up all creation are God's family—brought into being by God, nurtured and protected by the Creator. Today we see much evidence throughout the world that many relationships within this vast, complex web of webs have been broken. Still, Christians know that God's intention "for the fullness of time" is "to gather up all things in [Christ], things in heaven and things on earth" (Eph. 1:10), to heal the broken connections and to reconcile *all things, ta panta,* to God's self. Until the day we enjoy this perfectly restored world, the interrelatedness in God's creation we now see only in part provides a sign of hope.

4

# *Diversity*

## *For All of Us Are One*

*T*HE PRIEST AT THE ROMAN CATHOLIC CATHEDRAL LEADS A BLENDED liturgy in Spanish and English and preaches in both languages. However, in his sermon he never repeats in English what he has said in Spanish or vice versa, because he knows that while some in this congregation speak only English, others only Spanish, the majority speak both languages. In this way, he preaches the Word of God to people who understand either language, but those who understand both languages receive an even richer and more multifaceted message. This cathedral is located in San Juan, Texas, on the border between the United States and Mexico. Conscious of the diversity in this congregation made up of Anglos, Mexican Americans, and immigrants from Mexico, both legal and illegal, the priest uses this diversity to build a richness and complexity in worship and congregational life that would not exist without people of diverse backgrounds. Most important, this diverse congregation ends worship every week by gathering round the table and celebrating their oneness in Holy Communion.

## *Science and Diversity*

This Roman Catholic congregation highlights the theme of this chapter: the core value of diversity. Scientists in all disciplines agree that diversity is one of the secrets of life, because life depends on diversity. This diversity is especially essential for humans, because, as biological

91

organisms, we require diversity. One of the most diverse systems in our bodies is the one used to fight diseases, the immune system. This diversity is needed to protect us from all the different germs, viruses, poisons, and the like that we encounter. If the immune system could protect a person in only one way, that way might be compromised or destroyed, and death would result. But our immune system has diverse ways to fight disease. If one way is destroyed, the body finds another avenue to protect itself. Humans without diverse immune systems must live in germ-free bubbles, because the slightest infection would kill them. Without diversity within our own systems, we cannot survive.

Diversity among species is as important as diversity within our own bodies. Life on earth is extremely interdependent. We actually have genes inside us that come from other species, and other species have genes that come from us. In the absence of this diversity, we would not have as many genes as we do to draw from. This is one reason we should be concerned about the rapid extinction of species in our present ecology.

Most of us can cite examples of the value of diversity. When I spoke with farmers in the Midwest in the early 1980s, I learned that one threat to them was the move on many farms from polyculture, raising many different crops, to monoculture, basically relying on one crop to make a living. Farms also changed from raising many different kinds of animals (chickens, milk cows, beef cattle, sheep, and so forth) to raising one animal. When most farms had a variety of produce and products, if one crop failed or the price fell for one kind of animal, farmers had other crops or animals to fall back on.

While we are prone to see the need for diversity in biology, in fact, monoculture is a problem in many areas. Computer operating systems are an example. It is obvious that computers are crucial to the infrastructure of the so-called first world countries. "As time passes, all societal functions become more deeply dependent on them: power infrastructure, food distribution, air traffic control, emergency services, banking, telecommunications, and virtually every other large scale endeavor is today coordinated and controlled by networked computers."[1] However, a software "monoculture" is held by Microsoft Windows, an operating system that controls 94 to 97 percent of the software in the United States and around the world.[2] In addition to stifling creative alternatives, the ubiquity of Windows means that the world's computers are all vulnerable to the same viruses and worms at the same time. Monocultures are extremely sensitive to attack, and costs from viruses and worms are over 100 billion dollars a year.[3] More worrisome is the fact that the world's critical infrastructure could be disrupted in a single blow.[4] The solution, according to many computer security experts, is to break Microsoft's monopoly by using other options, such as Apple or Linux. Even within a single operating system, computer security people seek to add diversity by using alternative Internet browsers, such as Firefox or Opera. Diversity is the key to security.

## *The Biblical Claim for Diversity*

The necessity of diversity is not just a scientific principle about the way the world works. It is a basic biblical and theological concept. One aspect of this concept is that humans are created as social creatures, made to survive and indeed flourish in community. Remember the creation story of Genesis 2. "The LORD God said, 'It is not good that man should be alone; I will make him a helper [companion] as his partner'" (v. 18). Then God created all the animals and birds, so man could live in community with them. But man was still lonely, because he did not have a partner as his equal. Thus, the Lord God put man into a deep sleep, and out of man's bony inner part, God created his partner, "woman." The formation of all human relationships is the result of man being given a partner. In turn, all human relationships are based on the most fundamental community—a triune God who is community as Father, Son, and Holy Spirit, but who seeks communion with us as well. The reproductive capacity of the first couple led to the creation of all human community. Here also diversity is required. We know what happens when animals are too inbred or when an isolated group of humans intermarry only among themselves for generations. Living organisms need community, but it must be diverse.

A second component of the biblical principle of diversity is that God created and continues to create the world with immense diversity but not for divisiveness. We have seen in the creation stories that God desires community for all God's creation. We are meant for one another. Of course, the first humans were not content to live in community and to eat only from the tree of life. They insisted on trying to claim power by eating from the tree of the knowledge of good and evil. From that point, human community disintegrated, until God lamented the fact that God had created human community and sought to weed out evil through the Flood. But from Noah and his family forward, evil continued to destroy community, until humans tried to create a tower to heaven (the tower of Babel) where they could reign as gods.

God's next distinct attempt to create community was to choose a people, Israel, who would themselves exemplify human community and convey this example to other peoples, that is, increase the diversity of those in covenant with God. When God's attempt with this people also failed, God became human in Jesus Christ. In the power of Jesus's death and resurrection, all people are gathered into human community in Christ. This community is very diverse, as shown in the Pentecost story of Acts 2, where people from every nation could communicate because of the gift of the Spirit. But it is never divisive; it is a culture of connection rather than a culture of division.[5] The apostle Paul expresses the cohesiveness of human community in Christ, poignantly saying, "There is no longer Jew or Greek, there is no longer slave or free, there is no longer male and female; for all of you are one in Christ Jesus" (Gal. 3:28). The church, as the body of Christ, is to model and witness to both the diversity of creation and its essential unity.

A third biblical component is that every human is unique, possessing a combination of personality, abilities, perspectives, and skills that no other human has, has had, or will have. Death demonstrates our uniqueness. As we so well know, no other person can undergo death in our place. Death confirms our irreplaceability. In the words of philosopher Jacques Derrida, "It is from the site of death as the place of my irreplaceability, that is, of my singularity, that I feel called to responsibility."[6] Importantly, understanding our call to exercise responsibility by sharing our particular gifts and perspectives can lead to a crushing, paralyzing sense of accountability that results in despair. We know we cannot fulfill this burden as we ought. Hope in facing our death is found in the gospel promise that Christ died for us, so we might live both now and on the other side of death. Yet God invites us to live in Christ now in a particular way. God invites us to die with Jesus, by being baptized into Christ's death, so we no longer live to and for ourselves, but in God, who invites us to love God by serving others. Living out our vocation is important for this world, because no other person has or will have our particular gifts. Christian life is always both/and. We share many gifts with others, and we join with others to participate in our common vocation. But we also have unique gifts that only we can contribute to the community—so no one else's vocation is exactly identical to ours. We are irreplaceable.[7]

## Diversity and the Congregation

The worth of every human is a principle recognized not just within the church but by many observers viewing humans from a secular perspective. When we allow all people access to the table to help design and contribute toward a goal, then the fullest diversity exists. American philosopher and educational reformer John Dewey explained, "While what we call intelligence can be distributed in unequal amounts, it is the democratic faith that it is sufficiently general so that each individual has something to contribute, whose value can be assessed only as it enters into the final, polled intelligence constituted by the contributions of all."[8] When we reference Dewey's quote, we are not suggesting that intelligence (measured by one test or another) is the chief or most important quality people have to offer. Rather, the point is that everyone has irreplaceable gifts and perspectives that the congregation needs.

Hospitality is a necessary ingredient for congregations that seek to build diversity. Most churches are not very hospitable. Often the opinions and the actions of a core group of leaders are cherished, while the gifts and opinions of others within the congregation are ignored, particularly when their views are contrary to those of the acknowledged leaders, their gifts do not fit any available "slots" in the congregation's ministries, or their social class, race, or demeanor marks them as outsiders.

Genuine hospitality recognizes that diversity strengthens a congregation and cherishes such differences. A congregation is stronger when it has a full range of competencies—carpenters, electricians, plumbers, teachers, financiers, gardeners, quilters, cooks, seamstresses, entrepreneurs—versus a church lacking such diversity of human capital. Obviously, a congregation is strengthened when all ages are well represented. Beyond the advantages of diversity of skills and age, however, congregations also need to understand diversity as the call to invite and engage people across the imagined boundaries of culture, class, race, and language. Churches enhance diversity when they are open to the stranger who is obviously different from themselves.

In Christ, not only are we empowered to cross these imagined boundaries, but life and energy are also created when we develop this diversity. When we count on every individual, the community that emerges is greater than the sum of its parts. Optimum learning occurs in great diversity. When we honor every voice, a much richer level of participation ensues. People are engaged when they are given a chance to contribute meaningfully to a significant goal.

Competitive individualism is a central idiom that has guided the people of the United States since its inception. But in recent decades, with the erosion of civic consciousness and involvement and the subsequent diminishing of community, this competitive individualism seems to have become more pronounced. At work, in interactions with officials, and in other public places, people often report that they do not think any longer that they are being treated as humans. Road rage is on the rise. Since 9/11 especially, Americans seem more on edge, more fearful. Unfortunately, the path of fear creates great opportunity for controlling and manipulating people.[9] The church remains one of the few places in our society that both provides community and welcomes diversity.

Our society has many clubs, or communities, of like-minded people: hunters belong to a gun club, golfers belong to a golf course, readers belong to a book club, dog lovers belong to a kennel club, Harley Davidson riders belong to a local Harley club, knitters belong to a knitting club, and so on. The list is almost endless, and there is nothing wrong with these groups. In fact, we authors belong to such groups. For many people these groups have replaced church. Yet the church offers what these other organizations cannot—an opportunity to live and serve as God's body on earth. The church offers an opportunity to live in community as God intended. Such a church frolics in God's grace, serves others near and far, immerses itself in issues of justice, peace, and ecology, and welcomes in its communion people of all races, classes, and nationalities.

Because the church is not the sinless kingdom of God but points to God's reign, no congregation lives perfectly as the body of Christ. However, many congregations are vibrant with excitement about being a foretaste of God's reign where there is "no longer Jew or Greek . . . slave or free . . . male and female" (Gal. 3:28). Other congregations seem to actively resist diversity. For example, one of the founding principles of the so-called church growth movement is the homogeneity principle, the notion that churches function at their maximum potential when "a membership is drawn primarily from one homogeneous element."[10] We strongly disagree with this principle. First and most important, it flies in the face of the Pentecost experience (Acts 2) and our oneness in Christ (Gal. 3:28). Second, congregations are not called to be social clubs granting privileges for membership, but instead to be the body of Christ reaching out to serve others in need. If the church is simply another volunteer organization of like-minded individuals, then the world does not need us. Third, the world needs the church to model a community that exists nowhere else. Homogeneous groups still maintain divisions between their group and other groups. Such groups use "we" and "they" language. It is just this separation that Christ is breaking down. Human wholeness comes as we experience and live out our oneness with all God's creation. Finally, as this chapter demonstrates, diversity in the church strengthens it both internally and externally.

The preaching task offers an example of the advantages of diversity. We authors advocate increasing the connection of the sermon with the congregation by having pastors form a pericope study group (or even two groups) within the congregation. One group would meet during the Sunday school hour to study the lessons for the next week and offer their insights into the meaning for the text to their context; the other group might meet sometime during the week. In each case the pastor would have done the exegetical study and would have reflected on the texts ahead of the class, but instead of "teaching" the class, the pastor would serve as a midwife or coach to coax out the insights of the members.

The more diverse this pericope study group is, the richer will be the impact of their perspectives. The Pentecost experience might repeat itself weekly—that is, people from different backgrounds will begin to understand one another and broaden their concept of mission—through this kind of group. Another example of the advantage of diversity is seen in the liturgy and music of worship. Again, diverse groups, representing many nationalities and celebrating the living Christ through music from their homeland, will enrich every service. Even congregations without great diversity in their own membership can be opened to God's Word in new ways by singing hymns from a variety of nations and traditions.

## A Story

What is the role of the pastor in enhancing noteworthy dialogue among diverse congregants? The different roles a pastor may perform in this process are almost limitless. We begin with a story we heard in one of our interviews.

> When I was in seminary, I thought that the position of pastor as leader was kind of the image of a strong-armed row master in a boat. I could row while glancing backwards to see where I was leading those on the boat, but I was rowing the boat out into uncharted waters, and I couldn't find a good direction rowing backwards. Then I was called to my first position as associate pastor, and I knew this image didn't work. Even though my brothers and sisters were in the boat bailing out water from my poor leadership, this image was bankrupt. I understood that I had never put enough trust in the Spirit.
>
> My next image was a sailboat, and the leader was at the rudder/tiller/helm, because I now understood that all kinds of people were capable of hoisting the mast and moving the boom and keeping the

wind in the sails, because we were all going together. After about six months as pastor, I realized that this wasn't the model either, because it still did not give enough credit to the Spirit. Actually, the place of the leader is not at the tiller; other gifted people can learn to steer. The place of the leader is in the map room, holding up the map so that everyone can keep in mind where they intend to go, for otherwise the ship is sailing randomly without a destination in mind.

However, even with a plotted course, when the ship is nevertheless blown off that course, as the Spirit blows the sails, the pastor needs to provide leadership in getting the ship back on course. But to get there, you can't sail directly from point A to point B; you tack. The leader often cannot know how far to go in the tacking by himself or herself and needs the help of others. The leader knows that unless the ship is tacked accurately, it will be totally blown off course.

Let's take the risk of analyzing this story rather than letting it stand for itself. In this story, our pastor learned very quickly that command leadership did not serve him well. Of course, there are times when pastors need to claim pastoral authority, when being consultative is not enough. There are times when the pastor's expertise is needed. One pastor likened such times to piloting an airplane that must land in fog. This is not the time to consult everyone on the plane for help in landing (although the pilot will consult with the other experts in the cockpit and those in the tower). Rather, the pilot uses his expertise to land the plane. But for the pastor, these occasions are not frequent. To be sure, a pastor can lead by command hierarchy, setting the destination, plotting out the course, and commanding that people assume duties to "make" the intended thing happen. But usually the only thing that happens is open or subversive rebellion! Only in cases of command hierarchy is diversity not important.

Notice also that in the story above there is the need for a leader. Purposeful ministry simply does not happen without a leader. In congregations, the pastor is almost always *a* key leader. Occasionally, the pastor will not be *the* leader but will support the work of those who have stepped up as leaders. However, in our experience, pastoral leadership at least sets the tone for what is acceptable and unacceptable.

In this vein, the pastor can function as a restrictive gatekeeper. Pastors almost always have the power to keep things from happening and can effectively thwart efforts to bring about diversity and change.

What this story implies is that the most effective leaders will move toward participatory leadership. Yes, the pastor needs to be in the chart room, holding up the map with the destination that he and the other leaders have set for the church. But when the church is blown off course and needs to tack, then the pastor had better be working consultatively with the others in the map room—and the more diverse this group the better—to plot a direction. Help is needed, because it is seldom easy to plot a tack direction that will bring them back on course.

Even while pastors must be leaders, we need to understand that "leaders must give up the view that there's one way or a perfect way to lead a congregation."[11] Leaders have a preferred style, and effective pastors will be able to articulate this style to others. They have to reflect upon and develop language to express clearly their thoughts about categories, including systems theory, various congregational theories, and leadership styles (transactional and transformational, for example). But the best leaders will vary their style depending on the issue, the people involved, and the importance of a situation or activity to the mission of Christ, and they will modify their style depending on the context and the diversity of people involved. In other words, pastors need multiple images for being a leader.

## Images for Pastoral Leadership

A fine treatment of images for leadership comes from pastoral theologian Nancy Ramsey in her article "Metaphors for Ministry: Normative Images for Pastoral Practice," which incorporates a vision for ministry from Isaiah 61 and Ephesians 4.[12] In this article, Ramsey addresses what she sees as a crisis in exercising authority and power in the practice of ministry, when participatory leadership rather than command leadership is the style:

> While it is important to critique clericalism's domination of parishioners, when shared ministry is embraced uncritically without

an appreciation for different gifts and tasks, chaos reigns. Some designated as religious leaders so elevate the value of authenticity that they think they need only to be genuine and, therefore, disavow any claim to the exercise of power in ministerial relationships.[13]

Ramsey seeks to construct an appropriate understanding of power and authority in ministerial leadership that also dismantles the patriarchal ideologies that have overlaid biblical insights about ministry. Ultimate power resides in the congregation itself and is conferred by the community on its members according to a person's gifts and the community's needs. "Here legitimated power emerges from a web of relationships and is entrusted as authority to an individual for the well-being of the whole. This relational authority values the interdependence of life in community—the compassionate obligation to each other into which Christ invites us."[14]

Understandably, Ramsey says there is nothing easy about such authority, because in the present church culture, the predominant image of the leader is unilateral power that shapes and influences another. Much church growth literature projects the pastor as the one who both needs dictatorial power and casts the vision the congregation will follow. This position comes from a worldview that is hierarchical, presumes inequality, and values autonomy at the expense of community. For Ramsey, power lies in relationship. Relational power "is the ability to affect or influence others and to be affected. . . . [Power is not finite but expands as] we invest ourselves in mutually enhancing relationships. . . . In communities of compassionate obligation, power is not exercised over another but in behalf of each other."[15] Ramsey wants to find metaphors that reinforce this view of leadership, realizing with ethicist Karen Lebacqz that the "values, ideals, and identity shaping our character will so determine what we see as true that it will predispose how we act."[16] Therefore, metaphors help shape our practice of religious leadership.

No single metaphor can describe ministerial leadership adequately. "In ministerial relationships dynamics of power, authority, responsibility, and identity can vary dramatically."[17] Therefore, the church needs a cluster of metaphors for ministry, all of which demonstrate relational power and authority. The four Ramsey chooses are midwifery, service, friendship, and shepherding. Ramsey acknowledges that this list is not exhaustive; she also considered the metaphor of gardener. But she concluded that these four are central motifs for a relational vision of ministry.

*Midwifery.* Midwifery demonstrates relational leadership in that the midwife can coach the mother but cannot birth the baby for her. That is, leadership in this metaphor is "ministry of tending to and encouraging others to claim their gifts and nurturing those gifts toward fruition."[18] Ministry, like giving birth, is hard, messy, and fraught with ambiguities. While some church consultants use the word *coach* for this metaphor, midwifery has the advantage of being not only a biblical image, but more central to life than a sport. The limitation of this metaphor is the absence of clarity about accountability for one's power.

*Servanthood.* Servanthood is a familiar metaphor for leadership with deep biblical roots especially in prophets such as Isaiah and in Jesus's words and deeds. Servant leadership is a biblical vision for relational authority that suggests "the appropriate exercise of power and accountability . . . and helps in discerning what is truthful and important in this place."[19] While Ramsey does not elaborate on this sentence, we take it to mean that servanthood suggests that those who serve are in the best position to know what is really going on and what service is essential. The first danger in the image is that servanthood has been co-opted by patriarchal values, so that those in authority subordinate others, and service becomes oppressive to women and minorities who have often been urged to accept subservience in the guise of service. Its second limitation is that it "presumes the one choosing to serve already has a sufficient sense of self to experience the choice to serve as freeing."[20]

*Friendship.* Friendship is a metaphor for leadership in ministry, because it enhances each party through the reciprocity of care, encouragement, love, and support. The only authority for the power of friendship is these bonds of trust and love. Thus, this metaphor joins love and power. Ramsey quotes ethicist Beverly Harrison, who describes ministry as friendship, "the most basic of all the works of love—the work of human communication, of caring and nurturance, of tending the personal bonds of community."[21] Seminary graduates entering ministry are often warned of the inappropriateness of "having friends" in the congregation. Ramsey expresses this concern by describing "the difficulty friendship has in accommodating the lack of symmetry in power between religious leaders and those with whom we work. . . . Ordained ministry is also characterized by symbolic and representative power, which creates an asymmetrical power arrangement."[22] But Ramsey finds this metaphor to be helpful in the struggle to talk about differentiated authority without distance. This metaphor honors the complexity and ambiguity as well as the dynamic character of congregational life.

*Shepherd.* The metaphor of shepherd "envisions the trustworthy exercise of power as care and protection."[23] This metaphor is based on covenantal trust that is illustrated well in Ezekiel 34, where responsible care and justice are joined together by God, the shepherd. Even in this chapter, however, those with authority abused this trust in their oversight of the vulnerable. So it is with pastors today. This metaphor demands our accountability in areas of professional ethics. "People share their vulnerability more readily at times of crisis, and this is when we are asked to exercise more power and control for their safekeeping. Shepherding is not benign paternalism but a temporary protection that intends to enlarge the power and well-being of all."[24] This metaphor lifts up the reality of power that accompanies religious leadership and discloses the dishonesty of a naive denial of power. It "calls for accountability to the less powerful, to our colleagues, to the church, and to the larger culture."[25]

Congregations that encourage diversity in all life and ministry will want to be led by pastors who adopt multiple metaphors to guide them in leadership and who understand the strengths and dangers of each metaphor exercised in isolation. The combination of these four metaphors does not exhaust the possibilities of images for leadership but does represent core images sufficient for a faithful vision of religious leadership that embodies relational authority and power in the congregation. As Ramsey points out, these metaphors insist on an appropriate exercise of power and accountability for that power, are congruent with biblical images of authority, preserve the complexity and ambiguity of the other, accommodate the storied, dynamic context of congregational life, fit contemporary experience, and help point to what is truthful and important for ministry in this time and place.[26]

So, the leader who wants to encourage diversity and who wants input from diverse sources will use at least these four styles of leadership, blending them depending on the situation. Also, this leader will understand leadership as participatory, incorporating a network of people working together to guide. As a result, genuine conversation among the participants is a critical need.

## The Central Place of Meaningful Conversation

We have established that diversity is a strength for Christian congregations and that leading amid diversity requires different styles of participatory leadership. Our goal in the rest of the chapter will be to develop strategies for encouraging diversity, beginning with meaningful conversation. Martin Luther described the church as a "mouth-house." It is through the Word that God created the world, through the words of prophets and others that God conveyed love and invited people to serve in that love. The Word became flesh in Jesus, and the church is fed by hearing the Word of God. Communication is central to the church. How do humans communicate? Juanita Brown, author of *The World Café*, responds, "Authentic conversation is our human way of thinking together."[27] We use "authentic conversation" as a way to describe conversation that is open, mutual, genuine, and trustworthy, and that honors the voices of all on important topics and situations. Meaningful conversation is a rare thing. It is hard work to listen intently and empathetically and to respond appropriately, even among people with similar backgrounds. When backgrounds are diverse—when people have different ways of thinking, processing information, and responding—meaningful dialogue becomes even more challenging.

We heard this message repeatedly from our scientists who spoke about the difficulty of communicating across scientific disciplines— for example, when astrophysicists work with biologists regarding the possibility of life in nearby solar systems. When these same scientists seek to carry on a significant dialogue with theologians—even when both groups are willing to work hard to make this happen—the obstacles to understanding one another are very complex. Still, the results are worth the effort. When scientists of different disciplines are able to attack a problem with the diversity of approaches they represent, the results are much more comprehensive than when each confines herself to conversation only within her discipline. And when scientists and theologians overcome their communication problems, when they can even work together to coauthor a book, the results are notable.[28]

Clarity about identity is always the critical starting point for faithful conversation. Church consultant David Ray says, "The church that knows who it is [or whose it is] and why it exists will discover the 'how' to fulfill its purpose."[29] We know from conversations with scientists that systems function best when there are certain things you can depend on and certain things are open for innovation. A system can be too orderly, which leads to an oppressive atmosphere, or a system can be too disorderly, and nothing can be accomplished. A balance of order and disorder works best, as we have seen in the first and second chapters. Once a core identity is firm (although in a continual process of modification), a congregation is much freer and able to risk by taking on forms of ministry that may fail. With a congregation of great diversity that is working for even greater diversity, developing a core identity is the only basis on which to proceed as one church.

A core identity is essential for authentic conversation to take place, and notable diversity within the congregation makes the need for such identity even more critical. Authentic conversation in any congregation is difficult to achieve. With a diverse congregation, the wise leader will take extra care to provide maximum opportunity for genuine dialogue to occur. The pastor has two questions in the back of her or his mind throughout the process of engaging in conversations to examine purpose and needed change. (1) What is the quality of relationships in this community? (2) Who is not at the table?

Wheatley identifies the basic task for leaders: "I think the greatest thing we have to do is to attend to the quality of our relationships, the level of trust for one another, and whether by our own action as ministers, we are doing things to bring people together, or we are doing things—intentionally or unintentionally—that are driving people apart."[30] The pastor also needs to keep asking whose voices are not being heard—the unemployed in our parish, the two-income households, the wealthy, the children in our congregation and neighborhood, or ethnic minorities in the area. At the core of mission in participatory leadership is the need to get everyone to the table and to encourage each one to share his or her voice.

Focusing on relationships is essential, because all change involves loss and can lead to conflict.[31] However, the reality of loss can be mitigated by caring relationships and trust. Change in congregations is necessary for at least two reasons: (1) Constant changes in the environment—from the community in which the church is located to worldwide changes—require change in the congregational system if it is to remain healthy. (2) No congregation perfectly exhibits signs of the kingdom, so congregations need to be about changing into a more faithful representation of the reign of God, even though congregations will never reach this goal. Rather, at its best, the church is a foretaste of the kingdom of God. Diversity itself is not the cause for conflict; sin is. Because of sin, leaders need to expect crises and the murmurings of the people around the issue of diversity, and they need to sort out illegitimate from legitimate complaints.[32]

Diversity, however, does mean that communication can be more complicated. All of us who are married, and even those of us who shared a bunk with another in the army or lived with a roommate for four years of college, learn very quickly that we have different ways of patterning our daily lives learned in our families of origin. Those who marry someone from a different culture understand that their communication has to be better than average, because habits for daily living and attitudes toward parents, child training, holidays, and so forth are different. The rewards for being part of a diverse community are great, but the challenges are greater.

Therefore, a community of diversity will have to be more intentional about its conversations and listen even more carefully. One group that has gained many insights into ways to enjoy meaningful conversation with diverse people is the World Café Community.[33] The organization "is founded on the assumption that people have the capacity to work together, *no matter who they* are."[34] Moreover, this tenet frees their work from the focus on personality types, learning styles, emotional intelligence—typologies we use to preidentify and

prejudge people.[35] The organization does not need to put its emphasis on constructing the "right" group, but to learn to converse well in
groups of extraordinary diversity.

## A Talking Piece

Bill has led immersion experiences to the Mexico City area for the past
fifteen years. Several years ago, a new director at the Lutheran Center
there used a beautiful obsidian turtle to enhance conversation among
our students. When we met in a large circle to process and dialogue
about new experiences, the only person who could talk was the person
holding the turtle. When this person was finished with her comments,
she would place the turtle back on the low table around which we
were gathered. A person could pick up the conversation and add new
insights simply by picking up the turtle.

Bill was amazed to see several things occur when conversations
were held in this way. First, the whole conversation slowed down.
People were freer to listen more intently to the speaker because they
were not thinking about how quickly they could interject their own
comments. The more verbal people could not dominate the conversation as readily as in most conversations, because it would be very
obvious if the same person kept picking up the turtle. Also, the group
was much more careful to ensure that every group member was given
the opportunity to contribute, although no one was forced to verbalize
his or her thoughts. In his classes, Bill sometimes uses the same methodology when his classes divide into small groups but with another
object instead of an obsidian turtle. Only recently did he learn that the
World Café Community has been using the "talking piece" for years
to strengthen communication.[36]

Intentional conversation is not a technique to relieve all tension,
and we want to keep in mind that tension can be very creative. A good
leader has the capacity to sustain ambiguity (or, as it is sometimes
called, dialectical tension). To be significant, dialogue needs to establish a baseline where everyone is open to change. As we know, change
brings anxiety into people's psyches. At times this anxiety boils over to
active resistance to the dialogical process surrounding the probability

of change. The World Café Community has learned to ask a hard question at this point: "'Is this not working, or is it just uncomfortable?' Sometimes the uncomfortable is necessary to break through to new thinking and new knowledge."[37] Some parishioners will be unhappy with this whole process. They prefer a pastor who will tell them how to live as Christians, and they will feel free to follow or ignore what the pastor says.

Participatory leadership means, in part, the loss of an "outside expert." Congregants "are being asked to actively contribute their *own* expertise and knowledge" and to suggest outcomes to be expected when real dialogue occurs.[38] Being asked to take responsibility for the ministry instead of foisting it on the pastor disturbs some parishioners. We occasionally see this phenomenon in the seminary classroom. As professors have evolved their teaching style from straight lecture to presentation intertwined with dialogue with students, and as teachers have instituted more small group work, a few students, especially second-career students, have complained to the professors, the dean, and even the president that they did not come to school to hear the ignorance of their fellow students, that they came to learn from the expertise of the professor. That is, some students, and some parishioners, prefer to be passive recipients rather than contribute to a community's insights and ministry.

The World Café Community has discovered the benefit of asking for a participant's contribution rather than individual participation. Focus on individual participation can lead to an overemphasis on the *I*. "*I'm* voicing my opinions. *I'm* speaking up. *I'm* participating. In contrast, focusing on contribution creates a *relationship* between the I and the *we*."[39] As the Café sought to build community, they "found that honoring and encouraging each person's unique contribution seem[ed] more compelling than focusing on either participation or empowerment."[40] The purpose of the group is not to criticize, but to contribute. One World Café member thinks of these conversations as being similar to potluck dinners:

> Contributing your unique dish is what makes a potluck so interesting, fun, and nourishing. It's always a surprise. If you simply come to partake of the potluck without bringing your unique contribution to the party, how can the party happen? In a Café conversation, each

member brings his or her personal contribution to the collective potluck of ideas and insights which enriches the intelligence of the larger whole.[41]

Now, if there is one thing most congregations are very good at, it is potluck! Here is an image of great value in congregations to communicate the value of every member's voice, especially in a community with significant diversity.

Wheatley and the World Café Community both focus on the best in people. Wheatley tells us that she is very aware of evil in the world but that she does not focus on it. She suggests that when you focus on evil, you end up being afraid, becoming defensive and aggressive toward those who are perceived as evil. "Whereas if you're really trying to work for the best qualities of humans, you end up with a much more dynamic, entrepreneurial, loving society."[42] One way to foster meaningful conversations for participatory leadership amid diversity is through the tool called "appreciative inquiry."

## *Appreciative Inquiry*

Appreciative inquiry (AI) focuses on the positive by searching for the best in people, their organizations, and the relevant world around them.[43] It focuses on the "systematic discovery of what gives 'life' to a living system when it is most alive, most effective, and most constructively capable in economic, ecological and human terms."[44] Its methodology for achieving this discovery is to ask the "unconditional positive question," thereby heightening positive potential. By focusing on positive questions, AI fosters "imagination and innovation; instead of negation, criticism, and spiraling diagnosis, there is discovery, dream and design."[45] Questions and dialogue that affirm the other bring change.

One of our consultants said that when you look back at the major changes that have happened in the world, they started with a conversation. The fall of the Berlin Wall is an example. A sweeping change, such as the Berlin Wall collapse, starts with a meaningful conversation, focuses on relationship, and asks, "How can our situation be different from what it is?" Such a question, this consultant continued, is based

on the premise of starting at the other end. It means taking time literally to think about how this world would be different if we were living
in peace and mutual respect among nations. Imagine what headlines
would look like or what would be reported on TV amid peace and
respect among nations.

The church is a place where we could help people start at the other
end. How would a person's everyday reading of life be different if this
person started by conceiving of the world living in peace and respect?
We do not spend much time doing this. Instead, we wring our hands
and say, "Isn't this awful?" The problem, the consultant added, is that
we think of the church as a machine. If we can find what is wrong
with it, then we can fix it. But appreciative inquiry says we are talking
about a living being with potential for a different future, like a child
with musical gifts who is encouraged (but not forced) to realize her
or his gifts by being given every opportunity to succeed. Both children
and adults would be much better off attending to their gifts rather
than their deficits and trying to build on their strengths. We would
be better off thinking of the church as a living, organic system where
all things are possible instead of just trying to fix a deficit. The church
that focuses on problem solving and the difficult presenting issue often
seems to get worse.

The focus of appreciative inquiry is always on constructive
dia-logue rather than destructive diatribe.[46] Nevertheless, deep conversations, especially among diverse people, will surface differences
of opinion and understanding as part of the effort to generate new
insights, however positive the intentions. Sometimes conversations are
not just uncomfortable, they get stuck; any evolution of the conversation grinds to a halt. The World Café suggests three sentence starters
that may help move the conversation along:

- What I heard you say that I appreciated is . . .
- What I heard that challenged my thinking is . . .
- To better understand your perspective, I'd like to ask you . . .[47]

We would add one other step that is prior to and present within any of
these questions—the practice of prayer in meaningful conversations
in the church. For meaningful conversation, congregations need to

begin their conversations grounded in prayer—prayer that centers the participants on God's mission and the need for each one to support the other. By prayer, we do not mean the obligatory prayer with which most church meetings are begun. We mean teaching the discipline of prayer in the congregation, so prayer is the focal point of every conversational group in the church. Often the difference between congregations that focus on mission and churches that are immersed in themselves is the centrality of the discipline of prayer in a congregation's life. As we have seen, a relationship of trust is the starting place for a faithful church, and trust is exhibited in part through the ability of the congregation to hold genuine conversations. Therefore, appreciative inquiry is a building tool for healthy congregations, especially where there is significant diversity.

## *Narrative*

We recommend appreciative inquiry as an avenue toward meaningful conversation for change in any congregation. One other constructive approach that is essential when working with a congregation of diverse people is the use of narrative—encouraging people to share their stories and the stories of their communities. People learn from narrative; stories stick in our minds. Think of the extensive use Jesus made of story (parables) and the gospel writers' use of narrative (for example, the account of the widow's mite in Luke 21:1-4).

When people hear one another's personal stories, they understand each other better. Narrative leadership tells the story of the congregation to understand its past, interpret its present, and mold its future. Community members can ask one another questions, such as, "What story can you tell that will help us understand the needs in this town?" "What story can you tell of your own experience of injustice?" "What story can you tell of how you have been and are living in your baptism?" As Anne Dosher, a mentor for the World Café, puts it, "We cannot have a true connection when we're not open to the other, no matter what form the other takes. Often people do not know how to be open, to reach out to the other."[48] In the church the presence of the Holy Spirit, our experience of Pentecost, empowers us to this openness. A congregation that has a central discipline of prayer will be most likely to find the power of the Pentecost experience in its life and conversation.

## Political Facets of Leadership

Much of the literature on church leadership ignores the political level of congregational leadership and focuses exclusively on the interpersonal (God and leader, leader and people, community development) and personal ("know yourself") aspects. In this book we also deal with the personal and interpersonal levels of leadership. However, looking at congregational leadership through the lens of diversity brings the political aspect of leadership into prominence because of the multifaceted needs present both within the congregation and the wider community. The root of the word *politics* is *polis*, caring for the welfare of the community. Diversity within the congregation means there will always be members whose greater need becomes the whole community's concern. Also, more diversity within the congregation creates more ties to those people beyond the congregation who need advocacy for things like affordable housing. There is a direct link between diversity within the congregation and the need for political leadership.

Throughout this chapter we have suggested that the task is to get everyone to the table in order to receive input from his or her unique perspective. We have also suggested that the more diverse the group at the table is, the richer the conversations and the more encompassing the goals. We firmly believe this. However, as with almost all important concepts, we hold these assertions in dialectical tension with the fact that large change begins with a few visionaries anticipating a possible future that most of us cannot yet envision. Dosher says that "every societal change I knew of started with an informal conversation in which men and women—young or old—were witnessed and 'heard into speech,' sharing their dreams and hopes for making a difference around something they cared about."[49]

It is also important to hold both of these points of view in tension, because we know that, while we want everyone at the table, in the congregation, at least in its present form, only about 30 percent of the members will be willing to become involved in intimate groups of meaningful conversation. In *The Search to Belong*, multipreneur Joseph Myers, building on the work of anthropologist Edward T. Hall, argues that belonging is multidimensional—that people will belong at four levels, which he labels public, social, personal, and intimate.[50] Myers argues that all four levels of belonging, which parallel the different levels in which people related to Jesus in his public ministry, are legitimate, and that it is illegitimate to coerce all parishioners into the intimate level of relating. The point for us is to acknowledge that not every congregant will become a part of these intimate conversations. Pastors should not beat their heads against the wall when fewer than the majority become so involved, as long as everyone is invited repeatedly, all are informed of any decisions (and asked to affirm them), and most important, minority groups are included in the conversations.

Finally, many pastors and congregants will protest that the area or community in which their churches are embedded is simply not diverse. We hear this comment often from pastors of congregations in rural areas, town and country settings, and suburban situations. We suspect that there may be more diversity in the area or community than the pastors and congregations are aware of (especially different social classes). However, even if a community is not diverse in race and class, every congregation can become diverse by linking meaningfully with a congregation made up of people from a different race and social class. Such a partnership occurs among congregations all over the country. Bill has written in another book about such a situation in the Milwaukee Strategy of the Evangelical Lutheran Church in America.[51]

Critical to this partnership is the equality of both participants. Such an arrangement cannot be limited to financial gifts—the monetarily richer suburban church simply giving money to a poorer inner-city congregation. Rather, there must be an exchange: pastors preach in each other's congregations, church members from one church worship regularly in the other congregation, joint youth events are frequently scheduled, and much catechetical instruction is done together. In addition, each congregation studies the needs and gifts of the other church. If one church has more financial resources, the congregation may help the other financially but only with the understanding that the receiving congregation has resources that are needed in the wealthier congregation. We conclude that every congregation that does not enjoy great diversity within its walls would be strengthened in its mission by forming a partnership with a church of a very different membership.

Although this exchange works most fully when the partnering congregations are near one another, such a requirement is not absolute. Many denominations, like the denomination to which both of us authors belong, have regional area gatherings of congregations that have an exchange arrangement with a church body in another country very different from the United States. For example, Bill's synod has a sister arrangement with a diocese in Ethiopia, and Beth's is connected to the Lutheran Church of Christ in Nigeria. People within these synods who have traveled to and immersed themselves in congregations in the African churches come back transformed by that experience, noting among many other things that the churches there seem so much more alive than the churches here. The bishops and pastors from Ethiopia and Nigeria come to this country and share their experiences in congregations here. However, one does not have to go to another country for this experience in diversity. Congregations can yoke with sister churches in a different part of their state or region. The underlying issue is to diversify your congregation that it may be more faithful, healthier, and focused on mission to and from Africa, Latin America, and elsewhere.

## The Vast Diversity of Church

As Bill was driving noted Canadian theologian Douglas John Hall to the airport after a series of stimulating lectures, Dr. Hall observed, "The congregation in its present configuration most often seems to be failing. God may well have a different structure in mind for the church, but at present it's not at all clear what that structure will be."[52] His comment suggests that it is time for the church in the United States to open itself to radical change, not for its own sake, but on behalf of God's mission in the world. Pastoral theologian Michael Jinkins asks in his book *The Church Faces Death,* "Is there not a . . . danger to reduce the vast diversity of church, the ambiguities of this rich human-divine reality to a few neat (noncontradictory) patterns, types, models, paradigms, definitions, or descriptions?"[53]

The denomination in which both of us authors are pastors, and that we love very much, is in great danger, as are almost all old-line denominations, of becoming a fossil church. We are convinced that Lutherans have a message to bring to the American situation, but we are not sure we have the will to bring it. The astute evangelical American church historian Mark Noll said of our denomination, "Whether Lutherans are in a position to offer [any contribution] from their own traditions to Americans more generally would seem to depend on two matters: on how much genuine Lutheranism is left in American Lutherans, and on whether Lutherans can bring this Lutheranism to bear."[54]

One of the enduring problems of the Evangelical Lutheran Church in America is our lack of diversity. When the denomination was formed in 1987, our membership was 97 percent Anglo. We set a goal to become a denomination with at least 10 percent people of color or people whose primary language was other than English. Now, twenty years later, our denomination is still almost 97 percent Anglo. And while diversity is important in all areas—not just in the color of someone's skin and the language they speak—the lack of diversity in these areas is symptomatic of lack of diversity generally. Look at the clergy roster of our denomination and see how many names still indicate German or Scandinavian origins.

We mention the danger of our denomination becoming a museum church because we think many churches in the United States face the same danger. And so we ask, why not risk who we are so we might become more inclusive, like the kingdom we represent? Why not consider in prayer and conversation many different expressions of the church?

We have already encountered the principle that we cannot consider what we cannot imagine. Most pastors and parishioners cannot conceive of the congregation existing in any other form than the way they have known it. This viewpoint cripples their imagination, their ability to think of radically different models of the church in which diversity is a central tenet. Jinkins points out that the church throughout its history has routinely faced death.[55] In fact, throughout its history, one form of ecclesial life has diminished and disappeared while another has been raised to new life. "But to rise again is not so inevitable as the tide—it is an act of the divine—and what rises again does not always resemble what was placed in the sepulchers of the past."[56] A church that is willing to die addresses its identity, its vocation, and its responsibility and offers up its existence in the Spirit of Christ.

Later in his book, Jinkins examines three taxonomies for understanding the church, including that of Alban Institute founder Loren B. Mead's *The Once and Future Church*.[57] As Jinkins traces the argument in Mead's book, he concludes, "Mead's taxonomy yields a relatively simplistic chronological conception of the forms the church has assumed in its mission and ministry: the Apostolic paradigm gave way to the Christendom paradigm, which is now giving way to a new and as yet undesignated paradigm."[58] Jinkins says that one of the reasons for the broad influence of Mead's book may be its simplicity. What Mead's taxonomy misses, though, is the "dazzling array of variety in the forms the church takes, the ways in which we conceptualize church, and the manner in which we define structures, orders of ministry, and institutional life."[59] The oversimplified taxonomy Mead presents leads "him to miss or to ignore the one thing that seems most obvious about the church throughout its history: there are a multiplicity of forms of ministry that are coming into existence; there are emerging a variety of models or paradigms for church; and this situation is not unique, or unprecedented, but is the way the church is and has always been."[60] Jinkins wants us to understand that particularity and plurality represent the glory of the church, despite the fact that in every time and every situation, there is a contingent within the church who react to change with contempt. The church has always had an affinity for variety, for otherness, and for difference.[61]

Therefore, we challenge congregations to embrace diversity, one aspect of the way the world works, understanding that the Pentecost experience sets the bar for this endeavor. We invite congregations to risk their own lives by considering different forms of the church that can more easily incorporate diversity within them. And we urge congregations to remember that their lives do not depend ultimately on their competence, technical expertise, strategies, and long-term planning, but upon the power and faithfulness of God to raise the body of Christ from every death. A church that is unconcerned with its own existence but embraces diversity in order to fulfill a more variegated mission is faithful and very attractive.

5

*Process*

*An Invitation to Adventure*

"*T*HE PROCESS IS THE REALITY." BILL REMEMBERS THIS STATEMENT vividly from a seminary course he took in the spring of 1967 on the philosophy of Alfred North Whitehead (1861–1947) and the process theologies of Charles Hartshorne and others. Whitehead is responsible for the famous opening sentence above as well as one that precedes it: "Thus nature is a structure of evolving processes. The process is the reality."[1] As Bill reflected on our fifth basic scientific concept (processes are as important as things), his thoughts were drawn back to Whitehead and process theology as one arena in which to present the significance of processes.

In this chapter we will trace the basics of Whitehead's philosophical system to help us gather a perspective on the centrality of process. In a different arena, we have been aware that psychiatrist Murray Bowen's work on systems theory, and especially the work of Edwin Friedman applying Bowen's insights to the congregation and synagogue, are based on process. In fact, the subtitle of Friedman's well-known book, *Generation to Generation*, is *Family* Process *in Church and Synagogue* (emphasis added).[2] Thus, Friedman's work, growing from Bowen's insights, is a second arena in which we can examine the critical prominence of processes. Spiritual formation is yet a third arena in which to examine the importance of processes.

119

## Substance versus Process

As we noted above, most of us naturally think of *substance* as the primary category and *action* or *processes* as secondary. The philosophical basis for this worldview goes back to ancient Greece, where emphasis on *being, substance, essence,* and *immutability* won out over *becoming, change, process,* or *evolution* as the basis of reality. The champion of being was Parmenides (c. 515–450 BCE), who defined reality as what remains eternally the same, while changes we experience are mere appearances. His chief rival was Heraclitus (c. 540–475 BCE), who claimed that all reality is in constant change. It was Heraclitus who said, "You cannot step twice into the same river, for fresh waters are ever flowing in upon you." Parmenides' view dominated Western philosophical thought until recently, spurred on by thinkers such as Plato and, among Christians, influential theologians such as Thomas Aquinas.[3]

For *substance*, Bill likes the definition by philology professor Frank Thilly, because it defines the term so clearly and concisely: "By substance we can mean nothing else than a thing which so exists that it need no other thing in order to exist."[4] Therefore, substance came to describe the very nature of God, or, as Thomas Aquinas put it, substance is the category of God. The triune God acts to bring forth the world, but substance is the primary category and action is secondary. Therefore, "things" are seen as more real than "processes."[5]

In our contemporary society, the rapidity of change we are experiencing has led some to doubt the adequacy of substance theories to explain such change. Can substance theory deal adequately with change as a fundamental category of reality? In fact, the very way we perceive reality is changing. "Until very recently we were quite content and intellectually satisfied with the way Parmenides viewed the universe. There was an underlying stability to our institutions, our culture, and our lives. But in recent years, we are being confronted more forcefully with the fact of change, and with the fact that the rate of change is itself increasing."[6] The rapid rate of change has begun to create a new worldview. We no longer understand reality as fundamentally stable but as being in a constant flux, in process.[7] This is the way the world works.

## *Alfred North Whitehead's Process Philosophical System*

Scientifically, Einstein's theory of relativity and quantum mechanics have undercut the view that substance is the basic ingredient of reality. Without going into detail about these scientific discoveries, we can say that the theory of relativity has taught us that our position affects how we see reality, and quantum theory states that in its most basic (minute) reality, the universe is essentially processes rather than things. Whitehead was the first philosopher who understood both the theory of relativity and quantum theory and incorporated these theories in his philosophy. A British mathematician and physicist in England who was developing his philosophy when he came to Harvard in 1924 to become professor of philosophy, Whitehead formulated his philosophy out of his background in physics and mathematics. His philosophical system has been called "the most impressive metaphysical system of the twentieth century."[8] At the risk of oversimplification and distortion of this very complex system, we will describe basic components of Whitehead's philosophy.

Whitehead claimed that reality is made up not of substance, but of a string of occasions, not a static essence, but process. Reality is not constant substances, but a progression of events. Thus, process philosophy focuses on dynamic rather than static categories. In process philosophy the concept that "no one crosses the same river twice is extended. No thinker thinks twice, and to put the matter more generally, no subject experiences twice."[9] In Whitehead's words, "This philosophy declares that to be actual is to be in process, and that every entity is an integration of opposites—inner plus outer, past plus future, self plus other."[10] Of course, the integrating of opposites is itself a continual process.

Second, in process philosophy, what is permanent is not substance but relationship or connections. Process philosophy advances a relational model of existence. In our everyday world, we experience the importance of connections and relationships as the result of the explosion of new ways of communication and transportation creating the global village. "We experience more than ever before the inter-relatedness of people and things in our universe and the interdependence of reality as a whole."[11]

Whitehead called his philosophy a "philosophy of organism," because he based it upon a theory of "the real relatedness of things."[12] A purpose of his philosophy is to be processive in character and relational in structure. In other words,

> the process of integrating relationships produces reality. This process is dynamic, ever giving rise to new relations, new integrations, new realities. . . . Change pervades existence and change is a function of relationality. If relationality is the key to change in human existence, and if human existence is not foreign to the world and the wider universe but is itself simply part of the larger realm, why should not relationality be the key to all change?[13]

Moreover, every event is the inheritance of all that has come before, and that inheritance is what is continuous. For example, in family systems theory a leader cannot focus simply on present relationships but must understand what occurred in the past—a multigenerational view of process that brought things to where they are.[14]

Third, God plays a crucial role in Whitehead's system. His God is also part of the process. That is, Whitehead's God is neither all-powerful nor all-knowing. God, like humans, knows the future only as possibility. According to Friedman (speaking about Whitehead), pantheism is the view that God is in everything. Whitehead's view of God is not pantheism. Whitehead advocates pan*en*theism, meaning that everything is part of God. God is process, who is in turn affected by the creation God has created. This God is not theologian Rudolph Otto's "Wholly Other," but the process of the universe. Because God is the universe, God does not interfere coercively in the universe.[15] Furthermore, God cannot force nature to obey divine will but can only influence the process from within by persuasion and attraction.

Process theology does not envision God as coercive or punishing. If God is the universe, why would God want to hurt Godself? Rather than using force, God provides the "lure" or persuasiveness to entities in the process of becoming. That is, God is the lure that leads everything and everybody to their creative limit. However, God does not force others to become what God assumes is good for them. Finally, the future is wide open in possibility. In process theology the future is unknowable to both God and ourselves. Thus, there is a radical openness to the future, so that all that exists should feel a summons to be more, to move into something better. God is at work with a persuasiveness for reality to be "more."[16]

Process theory allows the church to move forward while "drawing from the deep fountains of the past, while responding to God's lure to the unknown but promising future, and while incorporating insights from the present."[17] Because of the nature of God, as Whitehead conceives God, Christian spirituality is not a path of safety but an invitation to adventure. As Whitehead himself put it, "The worship of God is not a rule of safety—it is an adventure of the spirit, a flight after the unattainable. The death of religion comes with the repression of the high hope of adventure."[18]

We are not suggesting that all readers become devotees of process theology. Some of you will reject out of hand any suggestion that God is not separate from and beyond creation. Others of you will express great resistance to the notion that God is not all-powerful and all-knowing, saying, in essence, "That kind of god isn't God." Many of us question Whitehead's view at the point of God's independence, God's aseity (having no source for existence beyond Godself). A panentheist, of which Whitehead is a prime example, does not believe that "God is a free being solely responsible for the divine being. God is not dependent upon anything else."[19] In Whitehead's view, God is as dependent on the process of creation as creation in its process is dependent on God. Many Christian thinkers, including your authors, reject Whitehead's vision of a God who is dependent on the process of the universe, because such a view makes process the ultimate being.[20]

We urge you not to throw out Whitehead's many contributions on the centrality of process if you reject finally Whitehead's dependent god, however. There is middle ground. We are drawn to the theologies of hope, first associated with theologian Jürgen Moltmann, as examples of ways to keep the emphasis on process while providing an alternative to Whitehead's view of God. One current theologian of hope, whose position we appreciate, is Ted Peters. Like other contemporary theologians, he takes science and the process perspective very seriously.[21] His own constructive theological proposal, which he calls theistic evolution, states that God creates from the future, not the past. God starts with redemption and then draws creation toward it. The world is still in process of being created and, when it is fully created, it will be redeemed.[22] Notice that Peters's position has a process perspective along with a view that God is not dependent on the universe. Peters also tries to include the insights from science in his theological conclusions.

The importance of process can also be seen in scientific inquiry itself, which is a process. As our scientific understanding grows, it leads to more questions, which lead to more insights and modifications of previous views, which lead to more questions—in a never-ending process. Said one of our scientific consultants, "Our scientific paradigm is in some ways like a pyramid. We build up our knowledge based on what we knew in the past and the way new findings change our understandings but don't completely invalidate the old view." Moreover, the future findings will modify what we think today, so the process is infinite.

More important, we agree with process theologian John B. Cobb's view that a process view of reality provides the foundation for living responsibly and transformatively in the world.[23] In an e-mail to us, Carol Rausch Albright reflects on God from the process perspective that processes are as important as things. She says we experience God in terms of activity: "*Ruach* (wind, spirit) is not tangible, but we feel it, and know that 'the wind blows where it wills' (John 3:8). God's action in the world is more mysterious than the wind (actually, so much more mysterious as to be on a different plane). But we experience God's reality as action, as what happens." Reciprocally, Albright continues, our response to God is also action. "To follow a calling is to commit ourselves to goal-directed efforts, which we understand as responses to God's action. We may miss the mark, but we are still trying to understand and respond to our calling. We try again, modifying our approach, and God in turn responds to us, so there results a sort of dialogue of events and responses." Finally, Albright asserts, real things—water, bread, wine—become involved in God's and our relationship. But "God's action is more basic than the tangible things. We need and have the sacraments because we need a tangible medium, due to the limits of our understanding. But the bread, wine, and water have no power on their own. The action of the Spirit is where the power resides."

## Family Systems Theory

Edwin Friedman recognized an intimate connection between his family systems theory and process theology. He writes, "I saw parallels between Family Therapy and Process Theology, not only between the major ideas of these two disciplines, but also in the way they framed the basic questions of existence."[24] Since its publication is 1985, Friedman's book *Generation to Generation* has had a profound impact on American clergy and rabbis. The nomenclature used by Friedman and Bowen, his mentor, has entered the vocabulary of pastors and rabbis and is used frequently, even by people who have not studied family systems theory. As we trace some of the basic ideas presented by Friedman, we note that he describes a leadership model that is congruent with the leadership model we are sketching in this book.

Leadership, says Friedman, is facilitated more fundamentally by the way leaders function within their families (or congregations) than by the quality of their expertise. That is, effective leadership depends on "the capacity of the family leader to define his or her own goals and values while trying to maintain a non-anxious presence within the system. Also, when it comes to *change* in families, clarity may be more important than empathy."[25] That is, being a nonanxious leader who can state lucidly what is actually happening in the family system is the necessary precursor to change. Self-definition is more important than expertise in leadership because the *emotional processes* working in communities control the direction of the community more than rational processes.

As a result, family systems thinking focuses less on content and more on processes that govern the situations, less on cause-and-effect connections and more on the principles of organization that give situations meaning. "The most outstanding characteristic of systems thinking is its departure from traditional notions of cause and effect."[26] Members of a family function not like billiard balls, but according to their position in the network or web of relationships. People will function differently outside the system than inside, depending on their place in the system. Friedman's five basic concepts of systems theory illustrate how different leadership is in his model.[27]

### The Identified Patient

The identified patient is the family member generally considered "the sick one," but in systems theory, this person is recognized as the one in whom the entire family's stress, anxiety, or pathology has surfaced. While families like to focus on this individual, the emphasis in family systems theory is on the overall relationship system of the family (or congregation). Further, systems thinking asserts that one must not look only at the present family, but also at the relational patterns as they have existed over generations—in the case of a congregation, the pattern of relationships over the decades. Friedman learned quickly that when one member of a dysfunctional family was treated in isolation from the interconnections of the family, lasting change would not occur. The issue would reappear. The reason is that the whole family—the whole relational system—avoids looking at the broader issues that contribute toward making one member symptomatic. Thus, the whole relational system is not changed, and everyone in it soon reverts to his or her previous position. Also, systems theory suggests working with nonsymptomatic members, because the symptomatic member may be so unmotivated to change that focusing on him or her (or on a particular group) allows this person to sabotage the whole program. The wise leader will work with those who have the most capacity to bring change to the system.

Friedman suggests that the tendency of any relational system to revert to its previous shape is the reason outside consultants so often fail to bring lasting change in a congregation. These consultants identify the problem (the identified patient) and recommend changes. If the leadership is very diffuse, consultants may recommend a more centralized leadership structure. If the structure is too centralized, with power in the hands of a very few, consultants will recommend a more decentralized structure. As a result, immediate improvement may be seen, but it does not last, because the consultants have simply recycled the symptoms.[28]

## Homeostasis (Balance)

Homeostasis means keeping the system in balance to permit the continuity necessary to maintain its identity. Family (including congregational) systems push to keep things the same, even if the balance is an unhealthy one or the balance was appropriate in the past but is no longer so. This concept helps explain the resistance to change that occurs in any family or institution (such as the church). Again, homeostasis takes the emphasis off personality and moves it to maintaining position within the system. Change always introduces anxiety. We have already seen that sometimes a family member or a few family members take on the anxiety for the system, and this iden-tified patient has a stabilizing effect on the whole system. According to Friedman, this patient functions like the trap under the sink that keeps out all noxious odors.

Friedman also uses the image of a string of lights to illustrate ho-meostasis. A string of lights can be wired in series or parallel. When lights are in series, as in Christmas tree lights, the current for each light goes through another, so if one fails, all fail. Thus, when one person in a system becomes anxious, all pick up this anxiety, and little change can occur. The hope for the leader is to have the family or congregational system act more like parallel lights, where each is more independent of the other.

In this book we have borne witness to the increasing rapidity of change and the fact that the only thing that seems constant is change itself. We know that constant change is reality. But at the same time, Friedman reminds us of another observation about change that, from his perspective, is equally true: "The more things change, the more they remain the same."[29] Because relational processes go back gen-erations, lasting change is very difficult to achieve. Homeostasis has a real hold, because usually when symptoms are treated in isolation, the underlying multigenerational emotional processes are not greatly affected. So, the fact that the only constant is change itself must be kept in dialectical tension with the idea that the more things change, the more they remain the same as we work with families and congregations. Thus, leaders must take into account the powerful emotional forces at work to resist change that would alter peoples' positions in the congregational network of relationships. Systems theory shows that effecting change is much more difficult than we would otherwise suppose.

## Self-Differentiation

Self-differentiation is one of the ways available within families to help overcome "homeostatic resistance." Change is possible because humans have the capacity for self-differentiation, some awareness of their position within the relational system. Friedman reports that Bowen "has suggested that a key variable in the degree to which any family can change fundamentally is the amount of self-differentiation that exists in previous generations in the extended families of the members."[30]

Bowen's definition of self-differentiation is "the capacity of a family member to define his or her own life's goals and values apart from surrounding togetherness pressures."[31] This concept is not to be confused with autonomy or narcissism, but is rather the capacity to be independent ("I") while remaining connected ("we") with others. Therefore, a leader's task is to coach a person to become more self-differentiated, which can bring more fundamental change than working on a family's weaknesses. One of the fruits of self-differentiation is the increasing capacity of the individual to be a nonanxious presence who is not reactive to the reactivity of others. Furthermore, because the self-differentiated self is always a connected self, self-differentiation is always a process rather than a goal. It is a process because not only is no one totally self-differentiated, but change in self, others, and the environment means that the way we remain self-differentiated is in constant flux. Again, we face an irreducible tension. This time the tension is between self and community. As Friedman asks, "How (in a nation, a congregation, or a marriage) do we strike the balance between self-sacrifice for the sake of community on the one hand and, on the other strive to preserve the self that makes connecting with others worthwhile?"[32]

An obvious conclusion is that families or congregations that function lower in self-differentiation are more likely to produce members who are quick to adore or be easily hurt by their clergy because these members are "fused" with their clergy. Such members are more likely to deify or crucify their leaders. And they are more likely to sabotage the continued self-differentiating growth of the pastor by trying to keep the pastor chained to their demands. A pastor needs to be aware that some members will so identify with her or him that part of these members' self-identity is tied up with that of the pastor. Because their identity is fused with the pastor, they are often the pastor's loudest supporters until the pastor sets appropriate boundaries on the relationship and acts in ways that seem, to the enmeshed members, to be antithetical to the "special" rapport. Then these people become the strongest opponents of the pastor. As a result, a pastor, especially one willing to lead change, will have resistors and usually downright opponents. Keeping everyone happy is not possible for a faithful, creative pastor.

## Extended Family Field

The entire extended family—including generations of grandparents, aunts, uncles, or congregational leaders now aged or dead—is important in the health of the family or congregation. Friedman urges us to "go home again" to gain a better understanding of the emotional processes still at work in our family of origin. A healthy modifying of these processes contributes greatly to our functioning in present relationships and in leadership positions in the church. This is to claim not that the extended family field is pathological but simply that this field has made you who you are. Therefore, the wise pastor and leaders will examine the emotional climate that has been inherited in the congregation they are poised to lead.

## Emotional Triangle

An emotional triangle is formed by any three people or issues. "The basic law of emotional triangles is that when any two parts of a system become uncomfortable with one another, they will triangle in the third person, or issue, as a way of stabilizing their relationship with one another."[33] Pastors and congregational leaders are becoming aware of how often they are being triangulated into a situation between two other people, or between a member and that member's issue. What we have not been so quick to realize is that if the pastor is the third party in an emotional triangle, it is generally not possible to bring change in the other two parts. Think, for example, of a spouse and his or her habit, which we continually try to change without success. The partner trying to change the habit picks up much of the stress of the behavior, and the partner with the habit is actually freer to continue that behavior. That is, the more one is unable to change the other, the more that one winds up with the stress for the partner and his or her habit. Triangles interlock and build within a congregation and then are reinforced by homeostatic forces in the system. The wise leader realizes that she cannot always avoid being triangulated into systems but spends her energy maintaining a well-defined relationship with each of the others and avoids trying to solve their issues with one another.

The processes of family systems theory are important as we think about leadership and change in congregations, because being more self-differentiated (Friedman says that no one is more than 70 percent successful at being self-differentiated) and being a nonanxious presence actually works to lead needed change in a church or synagogue.[34] Family systems theory has reinforced the concept we have been exploring—that leadership and change are relational. Because relationships are fundamental, one of the central issues in leadership is the building of trust in the system. Building trust in the system allows one to let go and see what happens. Only trust allows letting go. The leader builds trust in the system by being consistent, nonanxious, and self-directed. Of course, any such process takes a long time.

In conclusion, Friedman, based on the work of Bowen, offers a model of leadership that is different from other models because it values self-differentiation and being a nonanxious presence over expertise. This model also insists that a leader focus on caring for the emotional climate of the congregation as a whole and changing the system, rather than focusing on or blaming the malcontents. This model suggests that pastors need to pay close attention to the relational history of the congregation as well as its present ethos to be effective leaders. It warns about the dangers of emotional triangles into which pastors are constantly thrust (demanding that the pastor "solve" the problem between the two). Finally, this model realistically asserts that effective lasting change is difficult because systems (congregations) have a tendency to revert to their former state.

## Spiritual Formation

Margaret Wheatley writes that one of the greatest challenges for congregations is learning to live in a process world. "It's a completely new way to be. Life demands that I participate with things as they unfold, to expect to be surprised, to honor the mystery of it, and to see what emerges."[35] Although what Wheatley says is true, Christianity nevertheless has always been about process. For one thing, we are in the midst of God's process whereby God created, is creating, and will create the world and everything in it, including humans. Inviting humans to live in community with God, God instead saw us seeking autonomy from God and one another. When humankind refused to live as a steward community, God started a new process by choosing one nation to be an example of how humanity is to live in community with God. When this endeavor failed, God become one of us in Jesus. We responded by putting that one to death. With Christ's death and resurrection and the gift of the Spirit, God started another process whereby God's followers are to live in the church, the body of Christ, as a sign of God's reign until the end of time.

Second, we understand Christian life as a process that is both complete at the time of our baptism and ongoing until our physical death. That is, we are sealed with the sign of the cross and God's love forever at the baptismal font. But the baptismal event also begins a process that continues throughout our lives. Every day in Christ we die anew to sin and are raised to new life as God's beloved children. Our physical death marks our final dying to sin, and our resurrection is our final rebirth. The imagery is striking. We are immersed in water to be cleansed (even if we are sprinkled, the underlying imagery is the same). We come up out of the water purified by God. But every day we find ourselves drowning in our sin, and we return symbolically to our baptism for its cleansing waters. Process is indeed central to Christian baptism. Nevertheless, many Christians view their baptism or their conversion as simply an event, rather than seeing it simultaneously as a process. Once we see ourselves as Christian, we too often act as if we have arrived, rather than recognizing we are at the beginning of a journey of living faithfully. On the other hand, an encouraging trend that suggests we are beginning to understand our faith as a process is the increasing focus on spiritual formation.

The approach to spiritual formation has been changing since Bill's preparation for ordained ministry. When he was preparing to be ordained forty years ago, he experienced little emphasis on spiritual formation, beyond the urging of daily Bible reading and prayer. In fact, spiritual formation was not looked on with favor in the Lutheran tradition, for fear that such an endeavor might constitute "works righteousness"—trying to earn God's favor instead of living in God's grace, and for fear that participants might turn inward and focus on themselves. Today spiritual formation is one of the requirements for ordination. Now many ordination preparation committees insist on spiritual direction as a tool for formation. Also, classes and other opportunities for spiritual formation on seminary campuses are being offered, where previously there were none.[36]

In Bill's generation the popularity of psychology and psychotherapy was strong enough that many seminarians wanted to see themselves as "pastoral counselors" rather than spiritual directors who care for the soul. The faculty at the seminary Bill attended included an ordained professor who was also a practicing clinical psychologist, taught pastoral care and counseling, and maintained a private practice as a therapist. Few faculty members, administrators, or students even conceived that the seminary might have had a spiritual director instead. With no training in spiritual direction, most pastors could not teach spiritual disciplines, because they themselves had never been trained. The consequence, of course, is that little training in spiritual methods and practice occurs in Lutheran and other churches. Because pastors and lay leaders have found themselves unprepared for this central task, the communal work of spiritual formation has suffered in congregations. Presbyterian pastor John Ackerman observes, "It is my experience that few congregations listen to God's call to them, and few help members to listen to their individual call and nurture their ongoing relationship with God."[37]

Perhaps this lack of training in spiritual disciplines is one reason the current American attention to spirituality has become so divorced from the church. Americans do see themselves as "spiritual" and want to feel close to God, but most often this "feeling" is divorced from the institution called church and is a kind of free-floating spirituality—a private affair without serious content that serves primarily to help people feel good about themselves. In other words, people embrace spirituality in a dualistic (spirit/body) fashion. They think spirituality can be developed apart from the whole person, that person's whole life, and without community. Doug Pagitt, head pastor of Solomon's Porch in Minneapolis, points out, however, that working on spiritual formation actually includes "spiritual, emotional, physical, social, professional, and private aspects of life."[38]

One Protestant seminary's faculty has defined its understanding of spiritual formation as "the work of the Spirit who brings us to Christ and joins our lives to his, so that in the struggle and newness of life, we bear the image of the crucified and risen Lord and make him known to the world."[39] In this definition we see three things: (1) disciplines are needed in spiritual formation; (2) spiritual formation is a communal as well as individual task; and (3) mission is an essential aspect of spirituality. In a like manner, a pastor, writing at Bill's behest, described spiritual formation as "the overriding principle that governs the whole of our lifelong process as Christians, to form and mold us into the image of Christ Himself."[40] In his definition we can see even more clearly the need for corporate and individual disciplines. Few spiritual directors would want to specify a list of disciplines that everybody must follow but instead allow the freedom, within consultation, for the one being directed to choose those corporate and individual disciplines that suit him best. However, whatever disciplines are used, the wise practitioner will exercise the same diligence as serious musicians give to practicing their instruments.

In spiritual formation, one never completes the process. Even for spiritual leaders, spiritual formation is a process of becoming, not something they have become. A gifted spiritual director with whom we consulted, who has been an author and spiritual director for

decades, describes her approach, acknowledging that her guidance
may be refused:

> My spiritual leadership will be blocked and enhanced along the way.
> My task as spiritual leader is to pay attention to relationships—with
> God, others, the world—discovering their interconnectedness. My
> leadership must always be grounded in the Holy. It starts with God
> and the gifts from God—graces God has bestowed on us in relation-
> ship—rather than techniques. Of course, I and those I lead will work
> on being more open to God and one another, but openness begins
> with our basic dependence on God.

For this leader, the process of spiritual formation has only one beginning place: God and God's interconnectedness with us humans.

Moreover, spiritual leaders, like our consultant, do not operate in
a hierarchical, controlling manner. Rather, spiritual guides accom-
pany fellow believers on the way of discipleship by offering guidance
and help as representatives of the word of Christ. The task of being
a spiritual leader is also intellectually challenging. Part of the process
of spiritual formation is "that one nurtures the capacity and willingness to use one's mind constantly and consistently to bring the
fundamentals of [the Christian] tradition and practice into critical,
creative, and integrative conversation, not only with each other, but
with all one encounters and does in the carrying out of one's ministerial vocation."[41]

In the hectic lives of most Americans, contemplation and periods
of silence, which are a part of spiritual formation, are almost absent.
"One of the most disquieting phenomena of our time is the flight
from thinking, meditating and ruminating."[42] Contemplation is a
process that involves silence. Says Christian mystic Meister Eckhart,
"Nothing in all creation is so like God as silence."[43] Contemplation is
a process that helps people be not only "open to prayer" but "open to
change." As the monk Thomas Merton put it, "Prayer is then not just a
formula of words, or a series of desires springing up in the heart—it is
the orientation of our whole body, mind, and spirit to God in silence,
attention, and adoration. All good meditative prayer is a *conversion
of our entire self to God*."[44] Contemplation itself is a process sustained

by relationship—relationship in prayer to God and to the neighbor at the door.

Involving our future ordained and lay leaders in spiritual formation and equipping them to function in spiritual leadership is one process that will help the congregation change and renew. The mainline church in this country is tentatively tiptoeing in the direction of wider use of spiritual formation but has yet to embrace it wholeheartedly or to ensure that spiritual formation opportunities are available in congregations.

## *Becoming Process People*

Processes are central in the three areas we have used as examples: (1) the process principle in theology seen in Whitehead's philosophical system and the theologies of people like Jürgen Moltmann and Ted Peters (theologians of hope), (2) family systems theory, and (3) spiritual formation. Each distinctive focus on processes suggests ways in which pastoral and lay leadership in congregations might be different. In other words, when we urge a process perspective, we mean to invite pastors and lay leaders to be more "process people," that is, people who help set clear processes and then engage people in them. Church leaders have not been trained this way. We have been trained to design plans to solve the problem by creating new programs that will work. We strive to be able to measure our success and find it hard to live with instability, chaos, change, and surprise. Because we leaders think we know the right program to ensure success, we often label people as resistors (identified patients) or allies, and we dismiss those who seem opposed to our plans. Wheatley suggests that being a process person means being in the moment rather than hiding behind our plans or measures. It does not mean that we do not act with intention, but that we pay more attention to the process by which we create our plans and initiatives.[45]

We form into networks, or webs, but we realize that even in networks, our chief task as leaders is to differentiate ourselves. That is, we understand that powerful emotional forces of homeostasis are at work that make change part of a long process. Unless change is firmly embedded in the culture of a congregation, the community will soon return to its shape before the change. That is, we know that a system may change for a time, only to find that, because the emotional bonds were not altered, everything is soon back to where it was before. So we work on healthy processes over a period of several years to address the systemic emotional issues of the church family. Of course, the next need for change occurs even as congregational leaders are solidifying previous change. The process working against homeostasis never stops.

Wheatley tells us, "Healthy processes create better relationships among us, more clarity about who we are, and more information about what's going on around us. With these new connections, we grow healthier. We develop greater capacity to know what to do. We weave together an organization as resilient and flexible as a spider's web."[46] By attending to processes, we become gentler people, more curious and concerned about one another, more forgiving, and more open to change.

The Christian church in the United States is becoming increasingly marginalized. Marks of a "successful" church have been "reduced to tangible evidence such as size, market share, political influence, healthy budgets, and the creation of model citizens living the American dream."[47] One of the reasons the church is being marginalized is that as an institution, it seems so resistant to change. One cause for this resistance is the very weight of institutionality. A larger reason may be that the church has not understood that "becoming" is its normative mode of existence. Listen to the way Whitehead put the challenge:

> For over two centuries religion has been on the defensive, and on a weak defensive. . . . Consider this contrast: when Darwin or Einstein proclaims theories which modify our ideas, it is a triumph for science, because its old ideas have been abandoned. We know that another step of scientific insight has been gained. Religion will not gain its old power until it can face change in the same spirit as does science.[48]

With Whitehead's comment, we have come full circle from our fifth principle about the way life works—that processes are as important as things, back to the first principle from the philosophy of science—that the scientific enterprise is always open to new data. This openness to change is a hallmark of the vital Christian congregation.

# 6

## *The Center*

## *Where Trust Prevails*

*T*HERE IS AN OLD JOKE ABOUT TWO PEOPLE WHO ARE DISCUSSING the structure of the universe. One posits that the earth rides on the back of a large turtle. The other challenges, "And what does the turtle stand on?" The first retorts, "Why, another turtle!" Again, the second presses, "And what does *that* turtle stand on?" The first person, being rather quick witted, responds, "I can see where you're going with this, and believe me, it's turtles all the way down!"

We mentioned in chapter 1 that some scientists have posited superstring theory as a sort of "über-theory," a way to describe all known natural forces in a single set of elegant mathematical formulas. There are many problems, both practical and theoretical, with this notion—among them, that it is not testable, and it is hotly debated in some circles. But both the turtle joke and the superstring proposal point to a common human urge: to answer the question, where does it all begin?

Margaret Wheatley perhaps overstates her own case when she asserts, "In the quantum world, relationships are not just interesting; to many physicists, they are *all* there is to reality."[1] However, as we have explored the way the world works and implications for congregations and their leadership, we have seen that relationships certainly are key. The interrelatedness of all things is one of the central principles we have discussed, and complexity, diversity, and process all describe ways this interrelatedness plays out in our world. When we step back and look at the big picture, we are drawn, somewhat playfully and unscientifically, to this conclusion: trust is the bottom turtle, the ultimate superstring. More seriously, we contend that all quality relationships are built on trust, and no substitute can be found for it. Thus, trust is the center of the healthy, faithful congregation. Further, as Christians we believe we can trust others because God trusts us.

## Changing Perspectives

We began this book with one goal: to offer clergy and lay leaders a fresh perspective on congregations and congregational leadership—one based on principles from science that describe the way the world works and that will help faith communities more faithfully carry out the vocations to which God has called them. We also began with an assumption: how we understand the world affects how we understand God's work in the world, work God often undertakes through human agency. At the same time as we draw implications for congregations from broadly held scientific principles, however, we exercise a certain humility about our conclusions, because we recognize that the views of scientists, ever open to new information, are constantly changing.

Observers of contemporary culture note the great changes taking place in many arenas of our world. Already in 1989, business management professor Peter Vaill described the environment in which managers, educators, and others worked as one of "permanent white water."[2] In 1999 the total volume of information generated by the Internet was two "exabytes," or 2.148 billion gigabytes. In mid-2007, the Internet was handling that much information every hour.[3] Thanks to the forces of globalization, the world is flat, explains *New York Times* foreign affairs columnist Thomas L. Friedman:

> Clearly it is now possible for more people than ever to collaborate and complete in real time with more other people on more different kinds of work from more different corners of the planet and on a more equal footing than at any previous time in the history of the world. . . . The playing field is not being leveled only in ways that draw in and superempower a whole new group of innovators. It's

being leveled in a way that draws in and superempowers a whole new group of angry, frustrated, and humiliated men and women.[4]

As quickly and dramatically as the world and our understanding of it are shifting, however, most North Americans view our changing world from a relatively stable perspective. Without necessarily realizing our bias, we examine our experience through the lens of science. We assume the world is regular and understandable and that phenomena are potentially falsifiable and can be tested by some kind of observation or experiment.

Thoughtful people recognize that science cannot produce absolute answers to our questions about how the world works, in part because scientists' observations might not be accurate, given the limitations of both our senses and the technology we use to supplement them, as well as some degree of bias inherent in all observation. Science itself has been overturned in the past century and a half by quantum mechanics as researchers have discovered that some things we thought were true are not. For example, in the 1600s, Isaac Newton and Christiaan Huygens debated whether light is a particle (Newton's view) or a wave (Huygens's perspective). The twentieth-century work of Albert Einstein and others led to the concept of wave-particle duality, however, the theory that all objects in the universe exhibit properties of both waves and particles. Another long-held but recently tempered notion is that cause equals effect. While the principle applies in many arenas of human experience, physicists, engineers, biologists, psychologists, philosophers, and others promote a far more sophisticated understanding than what we generally think of when we watch a billiard ball smack the eight ball into a corner pocket. Quantum mechanics raises as many questions as it answers, but it is useful because, although it confounds us at the macro level, it explains many observations in the subatomic world. The point, however, is that in some ways, science is in great turmoil—flux far greater than we nonscientists generally realize. Further, careful thinkers acknowledge that some kinds of questions—questions of value, meaning, and purpose—cannot be answered by science. Still, as we posited in our introduction, science and its worldview not only must be taken very seriously, but may help us gain a new perspective on leadership in social organizations, such as congregations.

## The Way the World Works

We have focused in this book on five principles widely held by scientists, ideas so pervasive that we are willing to say, "This is the way the world—including congregations—works." As we noted above and discussed at length in chapter 3, one core principle is the interrelatedness of all that exists. Interrelatedness is the capacity for mutual influence between and among the elements of a web. That is, the world consists of not only complex webs, but dense networks of webs. Congregational leadership is better envisioned as webs of influence than a chain of command. Paul's image of the church as the body of Christ in 1 Corinthians 12 reminds us that all members of the congregation are interrelated and that each person plays a role no one else can exactly replicate. Congregation leaders therefore do well to be in dialogue and work with all the congregation's members.

An ELCA bishop who is a colleague of Bill's tells the story of an angry parishioner who verbally attacked him during an annual congregational meeting. The man ended his tirade by saying, "I think this congregation would be better off without any relationship with you." The pastor replied, "You may well wish to be rid of me, and I, in turn, might be happy to be rid of you. But like it or not, we're stuck with one another. In Christ, you and I are forever brothers, and this is God's doing, not something we can change." Our interrelatedness as brothers and sisters in Christ is a foundational aspect of Christian ecclesiology and needs to be evidenced in the way leadership is exercised in congregations and throughout the church.

In a broader sense, the principle of interrelatedness points to the interconnectedness of the whole human race—without *any* qualifications. In this sense, Christians are related to the whole human race, not just fellow Christians. Evidence of this principle begins with the creation stories of Genesis 1 and 2, and appears all through the Bible. Because God loves people of every nation, ethnic group, religion, and other category, therefore, a faithful congregation is concerned with all humanity. Finally, the interrelatedness of all things points to God's desire for all creation. Throughout Scripture—from John 3:16 ("For God so loved the world [cosmos]"), through Romans 8:21 ("the creation itself will be set free from its bondage to decay and will obtain the freedom of the glory of the children of God"), to the Christ hymn of Colossians 1:15-20—we hear the theme that God loves and cherishes the whole creation. Further, in a way that we cannot even imagine, God will redeem all creation, healing all torn relationships, restoring to wholeness all that has been broken. All reality is related in redemption as well as in creation. Thus, this scientific rubric, together with the biblical witness of God's intention for the entire creation, means that congregations are to live as stewards of God's whole creation.

A second key principle from science, which we explored in chapter 2, is that life is incontrovertibly complex, consisting of webs of active, interlinked connections. Scientific complexity theory is rooted in the concepts of self-organization and emergence: natural systems have a tendency to become more intricately organized all by themselves, and as a result, new, unforeseen phenomena occur. These creative processes are most often observed where order and disorder meet—when systems are open enough to allow for some disequilibrium. We see in our society and the church itself a pressure to simplify, especially with regard to the renewal of moribund congregations. As we said in our complexity chapter, however, simple solutions often turn out to be simplistic and bear little lasting fruit.

Loren Mead describes longtime Alban Institute consultant Speed Leas as "the guru *par excellence* of church conflict." In an essay, Mead observes, "[Leas] always told me that the most important thing in working in a hot fight is to recognize that everybody wants to simplify the issues so you have clear reasons for killing each other (spiritually, of course in *most* church conflicts). He said that the most important thing one can do is to 'complexify things.'"[5] Mead continues, "What he meant, I think, is that only when you begin to see new dimensions of what is going on are you able to get beyond dead ends. When you see all ten sides of the issue you'd mistakenly thought had only two, only then can you begin working out of the polarization."[6] Mead's comments perfectly illustrate the principle of complexity at work.

We believe effective, faithful leadership in today's and tomorrow's church must reflect the principle of complexity. As a result, we do not offer a simple set of steps for revitalizing a congregation, steps pastoral and lay leaders may crave. In fact, our argument is that most issues of lasting import are complex. Furthermore, understanding the complexity of a congregation is essential to carrying out the also complex calling to lead. Instead of providing a simple list of conclusions we have come to, we have tried to paint a rich, complex landscape—one that discloses increasing subtleties and deeper meanings the longer we look at it, that reveals the many different and ever-changing textures, shapes, and hues of both congregations and congregation leadership.

Another scientific principle we have explored (in chapter 5) is that reality is in constant flux, in process. Contemporary Scottish painter Paul Gardner is said to have observed, "A painting is never finished. It just stops in interesting places." The art of leadership, like a skillfully painted landscape—and, indeed, all reality—is not only complex but never finished. What is permanent is not substance but relationship or connections, the material out of which to weave a vision for the future. The Christian faith has always been about process—God's ongoing work of creation, God's unending efforts in Christ to reconcile all creation to Godself, as well as God's patient formation and reformation of Christians and the whole body of Christ throughout our journey with God. Yes, God is our rock, our fortress, our sure foundation. But we know God through verbs, God's actions and the movement of God's Spirit—through processes. Like the rest of God's world, good leadership is always about process and in process.

In healthy systems, the relationships central to process are relationships of trust. Such relationships enable leaders to have confidence in a process that is always seeking new information from the most diverse, and sometimes even hostile, sources. Diversity, then, is both a fourth central scientific principle (examined in chapter 4), critical to the well functioning of any ecological unit, and a basic source and goal of good leadership. The more diverse the sources on which leaders rely for information, the more closely such information reflects the real, complex universe God created and the changing communities in which congregations live. Therefore, wise and faithful congregations work to create a culture of deep, unifying hospitality. To achieve this goal, they move toward participatory leadership, exercising power on behalf of, not over, others. Once again, we see that the quality of the relationships within a system, such as a congregation, is key to the overall well-being of the body. However, diversity always remains a goal, because no community, religious or otherwise, is as diverse as the vision of God's reign, where the "wolf shall live with the lamb" (Isa. 11:6) and a banquet feast will be served from which no one will be excluded (Isa. 25:6).

Finally, we observed in chapter 1, the scientific enterprise is always open to new information, new ways of describing how the world goes round. When information flows freely within a system and between the system and its environment, the system is able to respond to change in its environment, thus preserving itself and ensuring that it is able to carry out its purposes. This attitude, one that scientists cultivate, will enhance the health of the congregation. In fact, when congregation leaders base their leadership on the implications of the above four scientific principles, these leaders are always open to new information. The mantra "we've never done it that way before" no longer functions as the seven last words of the church. Rather, congregations live with an openness, if not an eagerness, to entertain new information. In this way, receptivity to change becomes a defining characteristic of healthy, faithful churches. We have seen numerous examples of congregations served by participatory leaders who understand these five principles and operate in a way that is congruent with them. We think these congregations will most faithfully serve their fellow members, the wider church, their neighbors, and, indeed, all God's creation, today and tomorrow.

## The Role of the Leader

If we have accurately described the way the world works, what is the role of a leader in a vital, ever-changing system—a congregation that is faithful to its vocations? We authors believe the scientific principles we have explored point to a style of leadership distinct from the many varieties of "command" leadership in use today. Command leadership properly describes *how* a person leads—through a hierarchical chain of command. Some authors also use the phrase "command leadership" (mistakenly, we think) to describe *who* ought to be leaders, implying that leaders are born, not made. This version of Herbert Spencer's social Darwinism maintains that only certain people have the gifts to bring together divergent groups and focus on the future—by command. The scientific principles in this book contradict both understandings of this style of leadership as well as a form of command leadership that only appears to be participatory. Many pastors have learned to move away from autocratic leadership to a form of shared leadership whereby the pastor and select leaders of the congregation work in a much more democratic manner to make decisions about congregational direction. While working together, however, clergy and lay leaders (or more often pastors themselves) still often restrict who may lead. They do not include disaffected leaders; those on the margins—the young, poor, or uneducated; or simply those who disagree with them. They are unwilling to invite the whole congregation to imagine how a congregation might faithfully live out its identity and vocation.

Mead affirms what he calls the dialogical team model of leadership. The model, he says, assumes that change is the product of a group of people

- working together to discover what changes are occurring in the environment and what those changes demand in response
- assessing and improving their own abilities to respond to or challenge the changes in their internal and external contexts
- using the leadership of the people present and looking for new leadership resources wherever they can find them
- making the best decisions they can where they are[7]

We believe a specific understanding of leadership is typically at work in this dialogical team model: (1) leaders are key figures on a team rather than soloists; (2) leaders and followers are in a reciprocal relationship that empowers followers; and (3) authority is shared and distributed throughout an organization.[8] Writers such as Warren Bennis and Burt Nanus, Peter Block, Lee Bolman and Terrence Deal, Stephen Covey, Max DePree, Daniel Goleman, Janet Hagberg, Ronald Heifetz, James Kouzes and Barry Posner, Henri Nouwen, and Margaret Wheatley promote these ideas to one degree or another. For example, Kouzes and Posner define leadership as "a relationship between those who aspire to lead and those who choose to follow," and they assert "the outcome of leadership is a result of the relationship."[9] Like Nancy Ramsey, whom we cited earlier, Wheatley offers several "metaphors to describe leaders: gardeners, midwives, stewards, servants, missionaries, facilitators, conveners. . . . They all name a new posture for leaders, a stance that relies on new relationships."[10]

Mead admits that the dialogical team model of leadership at least implied by these writers "is undramatic and tough. It takes a long time, and there are no guarantees of success. . . . Such a team does not come together easily or quickly." On the other hand, "When it works, the change can be spectacular." Mead concludes, however, "I think this model is within the realm of possibility for most of us, and—let me be honest—I think it best epitomizes the kind of leadership God is calling us to in a posthierarchical world."[11] Of course, even as we uphold this model, we recognize that different situations call for different methods, or styles, of leadership. We are grateful that, should either of us ever end up in a hospital emergency room, the staff would not begin a consensus-building process to determine how best to address the crisis! Rather, one skilled person would take charge and direct the assembled medical team. Yes, each member of the team would exercise particular expertise. But leadership-by-command would be warranted, even essential. Congregation leaders may even command, as the situation requires, and we should avoid confusing *motivations and goals* of leaders with their *methods*.

### Where to Begin

In their book *Holy Conversations: Strategic Planning as a Spiritual Practice for Congregations*, Alice Mann and Gil Rendle demonstrate how a dialogical leadership model might be put into practice. One leadership dilemma they discuss illustrates particularly well the difference between dialogical team leadership and other understandings of leadership. Rendle and Mann report that Alban staff members are often asked "where the vision is *supposed* to come from in the life of a congregation."[12] Some well-known and influential writers insist that the pastor (or the senior pastor) must play the role of the vision caster in a congregation. Others insist with equal vigor that the impetus for change must rise up from the members. And yet others support what Rendle and Mann call "a connectional theory of vision formation": "The primary unit of mission is not the congregation, but rather the wider fellowship of believers in this region."[13]

Rendle and Mann propose, however, "The congregation's vision might be seen in another way—as the meaning the congregation makes about its present and its future." This meaning making is the "process by which people make sense of their faith lives—as individuals and as congregations."[14] They go on to cite the work of leadership theorists Wilfred Drath and Charles Palus, who "see the person in formal authority as one participant in an organization-wide process of the meaning-making that is going on all the time. . . . In this framework, leadership is seen not as a trait or an official role, but rather as a *process* in which people *make meaning together*."[15] They note: "We may say that spiritual leadership is occurring wherever members of the faith community are weaving new strands of connection between the source of meaning (as defined by their religious tradition) and their present situation—with all its perils, opportunities, and choices. The act of weaving, no matter who is doing it, *is* spiritual leadership."[16] The richest tapestry will be woven when leaders, members, and regional church leaders "generally concur that the model applied is appropriate" and thus are best able to recognize their interdependence and solicit the perspectives and gifts of the others.[17]

Consistent with this image of the dialogical model, Wheatley suggested in an interview that we do not need to worry about where the impetus for increasing the congregation's vitality comes from. "We really just need to start anywhere," she said. "And then, because we're in a network, we can trust the network will pick it up, and it will grow in power and capacity. Let's just get started and then learn from that experience."[18] Her comment echoes a basic principle in the work of family systems theorist Edwin Friedman: "With an organic systems model, the criterion of whom to counsel is no longer who has the symptom, but *who has the greatest capacity to bring change to the system*."[19] In effect, both Wheatley and Friedman suggest that "the vitality" or the one "who has the greatest capacity to bring change to the system" might not involve the formal leader. They also encourage congregation leaders—whether formal or informal, with or without authority—to go where the energy is in a system, to notice what is already working or offers a sign of hope. Like Rendle and Mann, they focus on the process itself, wherever it might begin.

"Getting started," to use Wheatley's language, suggests several tasks for leaders. In our first chapter, we said leaders need to help everyone in a congregation pay attention to the information flowing throughout the system and between the system and its environment, especially watching for information that will help clarify and strengthen a congregation's identity. In our chapter on complexity, we asserted that the faithful leader works especially to bring people into meaningful relationships with one another and God, establishing connections and sparking others' imagination rather than commanding and controlling. In addition, however—even in congregations that have identified and encouraged many members' diverse gifts, particularly their gifts for leadership, and that are open to change—the pastor has a unique role: the pastor is *designated by the community* to pay attention to the vitality of the system. The pastor usually provides a point of convergence in the web and thereby exercises varying degrees of influence, depending in part on the congregation's size. In a well-functioning congregation, though, the pastor functions not by command but as a leader among leaders, as a focal point in a leadership web within the wider congregational web, which is interrelated with many other webs, as we discussed in chapter 3. "Getting started" might begin with the pastor's influence, but it might also begin elsewhere in the web or even in another interconnected web.

## Leadership and Meaning Making

Another aspect of Rendle and Mann's image of leadership captures our imagination: leadership is "a *process* in which people *make meaning together*." A form of "meaning making" that has brought vitality to many mainline Protestant congregations is innovative engagement with traditional Christian practices.[20] In *The Practicing Congregation*, researcher Diana Butler Bass identifies a trend "whereby religious communities focus on meaning-making by gathering up the past and re-presenting it through both story and action in ways that help people connect with God, one another, and the world outside the doors of church buildings."[21] Bass further describes these congregations, in part, as "communities that choose to rework denominational tradition in light of local experience to create a web of practices that transmit identity, nurture community, cultivate mature spirituality, and advance mission."[22] Confronted with a new, rootless generation of Americans in search of a tradition, one longing for "faith-filled meaning-making in post-Christian culture,"[23] these congregations have moved toward genuine spiritual community by "re-traditionalizing" old and ancient traditions for the contemporary situation.

In some cases practicing Protestant congregations have reached into Eastern Orthodoxy or Roman Catholicism and retrieved practices that have been weak or lost among mainline churches. For example, a Lutheran church might learn a way of prayer and discernment based on the spiritual exercises of St. Ignatius of Loyola. Other congregations are inviting a renewed use of testimony in a nonformulaic manner. Phinney Ridge Lutheran Church in Seattle, one of the congregations the authors know best among those studied by Bass, has returned to the early church's practice of the adult catechumenate—Christian formation centered in hospitality and carried out through weekly instruction. The whole congregation is brought into this year of instruction—called "The WAY"—through periodic celebrations during Sunday worship of the catechumens' ongoing formation.[24]

The primary meaning-making practice may differ from one congregation to another, but whatever the practice, it has become central to the life of that church. As we have read the work of Diana Butler Bass and Dorothy Bass, we have been struck by the fact that in both congregations' practice of leadership and their broader life together, they exemplify many of the scientific principles we have discussed. As a group, they welcome new information—digging deep into their own experience, their environment, the witness of the church through the ages, and other varied sources of wisdom about God's work in the world today. These churches resist facile oversimplification of the Christian faith and its implications for daily living, an oversimplification favored in many contemporary Christian churches eager to respond to the demands of our quick-fix culture. They welcome the varied gifts of diverse peoples and are intent on "finding God's will for them both as communities and as individuals" as well as discerning "those specific practices to which they are called—the practices that provide coherence and meaning for their own unique stories."[25] They understand the Christian life as a journey—"becoming a community, growing in intimacy with God, and welcoming strangers,"[26] and they do not expect to find easy answers, solve problems overnight, or discover shortcuts to God. Most important, through the practices to which they feel called, these congregations give themselves over as communities to God's work in the world. Centered in God's trust in us, clergy and laity alike faithfully exercise their vocation to serve God by serving one another and their neighbors throughout the world—thus living out their essential interrelatedness to all God's creation.

## *Where Trust Prevails*

In our chapter on interrelatedness, we explored the idea that everyone in a congregation participates in an intricate relational dance—that for good or ill, every relationship affects every other relationship and the system as a whole, as well as other interrelated systems. The center of these interrelated webs is trust, for without trust, the relationships cannot hold. Rather than forming the dense networks of webs essential to a vital system, strands that are not centered in trust will be fragile and will crisscross chaotically, producing a weak, ineffective system.

The need for trust in faith communities is most obvious in congregations where trust has been broken by a clergyperson, youth director, musician, childcare worker, Sunday school teacher, bookkeeper, or financial secretary who violates sexual boundaries, misuses or embezzles funds, or in other ways violates members' appropriate expectations for leaders.[27] Clergy who serve congregations where misconduct has occurred in the past (sometimes called afterpastors) often experience distrust and suspicion; report feeling manipulated, coerced, and sabotaged; struggle with erratic and confusing communication patterns; and are faced with deliberate undermining of their ministries.[28] Obviously, these crazy-making behaviors affect not only the pastor, but all congregational leaders and members. Congregations where misconduct has occurred tend to exhibit general reactivity and participate in petty, perennial conflicts.[29] According to Deborah Pope-Lance, coach to afterpastors, the afterpastor must respond to such behavior by making "reparations to the office of ministry by exercising emotional neutrality, establishing clear boundaries, and rebuilding trust in pastoral relationships. . . . On a day-to-day, person-to-person basis, an afterpastor heals the office of ministry with every interaction that is truthful, appropriate, competent, healthy, and respectful."[30] Of course, the afterpastor alone, although designated to pay attention to the community's relationships, cannot restore *relationships*. Only by working together to restore trust can clergy and lay leaders hope to bring about the healing of relationships and, thus, the congregation as a whole, building an environment where creative, faithful leadership and ministry can occur.

The goal of creating and leading from a foundation of trust does not suggest only one way to lead. Rather, when a system is characterized by relationships of trust, leaders are given the freedom to exercise different styles of leadership, depending on the needs of the web to which they belong—and the webs to which it is connected. Leaders still treat their followers with respect, building on and further engendering trust, even when the situation requires that they exercise command. This way of trust and love is particularly consistent with another significant contemporary view of leadership most closely associated with Robert Greenleaf: the servant-leader paradigm, or the image of the leader as a steward or trustee. In his first widely distributed series of essays on the topic, *The Servant as Leader*, published in 1970, Greenleaf wrote:

> The servant-leader is servant first. . . . It begins with the natural feeling that one wants to serve, to serve *first*. Then conscious choice brings one to aspire to lead. . . . The difference manifests itself in the care taken by the servant—first to make sure that other people's highest-priority needs are being served. The best test, and the most difficult to administer, is: Do those served grow as persons? Do they, *while being served*, become healthier, wiser, freer, more autonomous, more likely themselves to become servants? *And*, what is the effect on the least privileged in society; will they benefit or, at least, not be further deprived?[31]

Exploring the image of the servant-leader from a specifically Christian perspective, the late Dutch Catholic priest Henri Nouwen reflects,

"The leadership about which Jesus speaks is of a radically different kind from the leadership offered by the world. It is a servant leadership ... in which the leader is a vulnerable servant who needs the people as much as they need their leader."[32] Teachings of Jesus, such as "Whoever wants to be first must be last of all and servant of all" (Mark 9:35), come to mind when we think of this image.

In one of his early lecture series, Greenleaf identified four essential "abilities" for leaders: values, direction, competence, and finally, *spirit*. He refused to define "spirit," insisting, "I don't know what it is, even though occasionally I get intimations about it." But, he went on: "I do have a belief about what it *does*. When a leader has it, it builds *trust*; it builds trust not only between leader and follower but also between followers. Humans have not always been trusting, but trust is the cement that makes possible institutional solidarity, from the family to world society."[33]

We authors value the deep impact Greenleaf has had on leaders and those who study leadership (and were especially pleased to discover he agrees with our perception that trust is essential to well-functioning organizations). As we see in Nouwen, the image of the servant-leader is consistent with Christian theology, which we of course also appreciate. We further believe that among all models and images of leadership, servant-leadership best captures the leadership implied by the principles from science we have explored in this book. Servant-leaders will encourage congregations to interact and grow in a manner consistent with the way the world works. Finally, better than any other understanding of leadership, servant-leadership promotes the development of trust in relationships. What we learn from the way the world works, where relationships are central, is that where trust prevails, leadership can take many different shapes and forms. But at its best, leadership is relational and, depending on the needs of the situation at hand, shared. The servant-leader image captures the essence of that foundational growing, trusting relationship.

## A Patchwork Quilt of Trust

The evolving, wide-reaching, community-building ministries of the Church of St. Philip, a Roman Catholic parish founded by Polish immigrants in the Hawthorne neighborhood of North Minneapolis, illustrate the power of trust in relationships. The parish's Patchwork Quilt Neighborhood Outreach was created to help area residents deal with extreme economic poverty, drug dealing, violence, and other challenges. But this quilt began with one small square of fabric. Shortly after Greg Tolaas was appointed pastor of St. Philip, he approached the parish council about opening up the church building just one afternoon a week to the children of Hawthorne so that the children would have a safe place to gather and something worthwhile to do. The council agreed, and Father Tolaas recruited several volunteers, planned a program for the children, and publicized the opportunity. The first day, three children showed up. So pastor and children went out into the neighborhood, hand in hand, and talked with as many parents as they could find to get permission for their children to come to the church. Within eighteen months, three hundred children were participating in the weekly Kids Club.

Among those recruited to staff the program were a number of elderly Polish women who each week prepared a meal for the children. Initially, the women stayed in the kitchen throughout the program, only occasionally peeking out to see what was going on in the fellowship hall. Eventually, however, they began to come out of the kitchen to talk with the children, and relationships began to form between the children and the volunteers. Father Tolaas always insisted, whether he was talking with members of the parish or residents of Hawthorne, "You can't just come here and be by yourself and go home. You can come here and build relationships. You can be part of the patchwork quilt." A decade after the program began, the church's Web site shows how the ministry, a patchwork quilt created by the parish and the neighborhood working together, has taken shape:

> The Patchwork Quilt provides stimulating and nurturing after-school and summer programs for children, as well as an active teen group. It also provides group support and challenge for often-overburdened mothers, and for men who seek better lives for themselves, their families, and the community. Begun in 1997, the Quilt is a gathering place for people of diverse socio-economic and cultural

backgrounds and has proven to be a news-making and noteworthy seedbed for growth and positive change.[34]

Other ministries have also grown up in the parish. Women of Great Hope and Vision involves approximately thirty-five women from the area who come together each month to share a meal, participate in an activity, and pray for each other, their families, and the world. In addition, as a group the women often participate in Hawthorne and church activities, such as get-out-the-vote campaigns, a neighborhood spring cleanup, the parish's peace garden planting, summer jam fest, and community Christmas dinner, Martin Luther King Jr. celebrations, and other peace initiatives.[35]

Another parish program, The Patchwork Quilt Digital Divide Initiative, connects the St. Philip network with a network of webs beyond the neighborhood, demonstrating further the interrelatedness of our world. The goal of the Digital Divide Initiative is to "provide computers and to improve 'technology literacy' within the low-income communities of Minneapolis." The program includes a computer exchange project, technical support services, a computer club for teens, and a computer-learning center for area residents. The initiative reaches well beyond Hawthorne, however. It is also a partner of World Community Grid, which joins more than eighty leading companies, associations, foundations, and academic institutions to solve problems and thus "benefit humanity."[36] In fact, the intent of the grid is to do nothing less than "change the world."[37] Using "grid technology," it links many individual computers, creating a large system with power that far exceeds the capacity of a few supercomputers. Among the many research projects undertaken, World Community Grid has provided scientists with data being used to develop new cures for diseases such as Lyme disease, malaria, tuberculosis, and AIDS. Possible future projects will address global humanitarian issues, such as infectious diseases, natural disasters, and hunger.[38]

The trust Father Tolaas practiced, the women in his congregation slowly learned to share, and the children, youth, and others in the Hawthorne neighborhood gradually began to sense and rely on grew out of the priest's, parishioners', and others' relationships with

God. Together they explored and nurtured this trust to create a warm, sturdy, colorful patchwork quilt. In part through meaningful dialogue with God in worship, the sacraments, and prayer, they have continued to open themselves to one another, developing new relationships of trust and stitching new pieces into their patchwork quilt. The people of St. Philip and Hawthorne grieved deeply after their much-beloved pastor's death at age forty-seven from cystic fibrosis. But still they sew with the strong thread of trust they have received from God and with new threads they have spun together.

## The Way of Love

If the scientific principles we have explored in this book do indeed accurately describe the way the world works, then we can expect to see certain characteristics in vital Christian communities like the Church of St. Philip. Congregation leaders and members who treat information as a source of nourishment exhibit *curiosity* and gladly exercise their collective intelligence in the mission and ministries to which they are called. Congregations that welcome diversity within their community and in all God's world develop skills such as open communication, appreciative inquiry, and story sharing—skills that help them practice *charity* toward others. Congregations aware that God's work in the world is to bring about change, to reconcile all things to Godself, conclude that as they live in relationship with this God of action, they themselves must likewise *change*. Processes often depend on complex webs of relationships, which tend to become linked in ever more complex entities. Congregations that appreciate such emergence celebrate their *creativity*. Ultimately, the quality of relationships—ideally relationships of trust among God, humanity, and the whole rest of creation—is foundational to the way the world works. Members of the body of Christ view themselves as both beneficiaries and servants of God's trust, which is revealed and *centered in Christ*.

This centeredness in Christ, which we commonly call "faith," is not a matter of mere intellectual assent to God's existence, reasoned acceptance of certain declarations about God, or even a decision to recognize God's acts through Christ to bring about the reconciliation of all creation. Rather, when we are centered in Christ, we participate in a *relationship* with God that begins with God choosing us as sons and daughters. U.S. currency is imprinted with the words "In God we trust," but theologically the phrase should read, "In us God trusts." God's trust in us—despite humanity's breaking of that trust at every turn—is the source of human desire to enter relationships with others characterized by trust, openness, and joy. Because our triune God is not only Immanuel, God with us, but also the God of *agape* love (self-giving love), therefore God's relationship with us empowers us and helps us create communities where people are woven together in loving, trust-full relationships that both compel and enable us to serve God and neighbor.

The Christian community in Corinth to which the apostle Paul wrote was torn by disagreements and divided into disputing parties—hardly reflecting the image of trust and love Paul held up to them in 1 Corinthians 13. One of the many struggles the Corinthian church dealt with was divided loyalties to various leaders—Paul himself, Apollos, and Cephas. Paul boldly addressed these factions: "So let no one boast about human leaders. For all things are yours, whether Paul or Apollos or Cephas or the world or life or death or the present or the future—all belong to you, and you belong to Christ, and Christ belongs to God" (1 Cor. 3:21-23). In other words, he told his audience, all these leaders are in relationship with the entire community and you with them. Even life and death, the present and the future are part of your world, the webs to which you are connected. All things are in relationship with you, and you with all creation, because you are in relationship with Christ—and thus with God.

Trust is an essential characteristic, the most basic ingredient, of the healthy, faithful congregation. In the end, anyone who builds trust—who helps a system form more generous, truthful, and mature relationships—demonstrating the "more excellent way" the apostle Paul describes in 1 Corinthians 13, is a leader in the congregational web. The good news is that as God's people, we can trust others *because* God trusts us. Better put, "We love because [God] first loved us" (1 John 4:19). We love God by loving others—humans and all of creation. Because interconnectedness is the heart of reality and Christianity itself is relational at its core, relationships are foundational for the church.

Quality relationships are built on trust, and no substitute can be found for it. Thus, building a trustworthy environment in a congregation is the precondition for creative, innovative leadership and service. This is the way of love.

# Notes

## Preface

1. Robert Banks and Bernice M. Ledbetter, *Reviewing Leadership: A Christian Evaluation of Current Approaches* (Grand Rapids: Baker, 2004), 50–52.

2. Margaret J. Wheatley, *Leadership and the New Science: Discovering Order in a Chaotic World*, 2nd ed. (San Francisco: Berrett-Koehler, 1999), 9.

3. Ibid., 24.

## Introduction

1. Carol Rausch Albright, *Growing in the Image of God*, Saint Paul University Research Series: Faith and Science, ed. Ivan Timonin (Toronto: Novalis, 2002), 13.

2. As we mentioned in the acknowledgements, readers will find unattributed quotes throughout the book. Our decision not to identify the individuals quoted stems from our desire to emphasize not the science itself and "what so and so said," but the insights we gleaned from their thoughts about science, congregations, and leadership. For a full list of our conversation partners, please see the acknowledgements.

3. Albright, *Growing in the Image of God*, 15.

4. "Philip Hefner Faces the Hard Questions: Ideas, Dialogue, Meaning and What Isn't There," *Science and Technology News*, November 1, 2001, 2, www.stnews.org/Commentary-2010.htm (accessed January 24, 2006).

5. Ibid.

6. See, e.g., John Hastings, "Modern Nursing and Modern Physics: Does Quantum Theory Contain Useful Insights for Nursing Practice and Health-care Management?" *Nursing Philosophy* 3, no. 3 (October 2002): 205–12.

7. Hastings, "Modern Nursing and Modern Physics," 205.

8. Ibid., 206.

9. John Polkinghorne, interview.

10. Ibid.

11. Hastings, "Modern Nursing and Modern Physics," 206.

12. Ibid., 207.

13. Ibid., 207–8.

14. Margaret Wheatley, telephone interview, May 10, 2006.

15. Margaret J. Wheatley, *Finding Our Way: Leadership for an Uncertain Time* (San Francisco: Berrett-Koehler, 2005).

16. Ibid., 16.

17. See Robert H. Kraus Jr., "Faith and Science," *The Lutheran*, February 2006.

18. Albright, *Growing in the Image of God*, 19.

19. Ibid., 36.

20. Ibid., 36–37.

## Chapter 1 *Information: God's New Thing*

1. Margaret J. Wheatley, *Leadership and the New Science: Discovering Order in a Chaotic World*, 2nd ed. (San Francisco: Berrett-Koehler, 1999), 96–97.

2. Carol Rausch Albright, *Growing in the Image of God*, Saint Paul University Research Series: Faith and Science, ed. Ivan Timonin (Toronto: Novalis, 2002), 60.

3. Robert Kegan, *The Evolving Self: Problem and Process in Human Development* (Cambridge, MA: Harvard University Press, 1982), 11.

4. Margaret J. Wheatley, *Finding Our Way: Leadership for an Uncertain Time* (San Francisco: Berrett-Koehler, 2005), 39. Cybernetics is the study of feedback and concepts such as communication and control in systems.

5. Wheatley, *Leadership and the New Science*, 93–94.

6. Claude E. Shannon and Warren Weaver, *The Mathematical Theory of Communication* (Urbana: University of Illinois, 1949); cited in Albright, *Growing in the Image of God*, 38.

7. Wheatley, *Leadership and the New Science*, 95.

8. Ibid., 96.

9. Committee on Science and Creationism, National Academy of Sciences, *Science and Creationism: A View from the National Academy of Sciences*, 2nd ed. (Washington, DC: National Academy Press, 1999), 1; cited in Terence L. Nichols, *The Sacred Cosmos: Christian Faith and the Challenge of Naturalism*, The Christian Practice of Everyday Life Series (Grand Rapids: Brazos, 2003), 200.

10. Albright, *Growing in the Image of God*, 19.

11. Ibid., 74.

12. Wheatley, *Leadership and the New Science*, 98.

13. Ibid., 20.

14. Ibid., 91.

15. Ibid., 83.

16. Ibid., 78.

17. Ibid.

18. Ibid., 85.

19. Humberto R. Maturana and Francisco J. Varela, *The Tree of Knowledge: The Biological Roots of Human Understanding* (Boston: Shambhala, 1992), 162; cited in Wheatley, *Finding Our Way*, 37.

20. J. N. Sanders, "Word of God," in *The Interpreter's Dictionary of the Bible: An Illustrated Encyclopedia*, vol. 4 (Nashville: Abingdon, 1962), 871.

21. Wheatley, *Leadership and the New Science*, 106–7.

22. Wheatley, *Finding Our Way*, 103.

23. "The GOCN Is . . . ," The Gospel and Our Culture Network, http://www.gocn.org/main.cfm (accessed March 30, 2007).

24. A Working Document of the "Developing Congregational Models" Team, The Transforming Congregations toward Mission Project of the Gospel and Our Culture Network, "Empirical Indicators of a 'Missional Church,'" *Sent Church: Journal of Missional Church Resources* (August 26, 1998), http://www.sentchurch.com/missional_church_indicators.htm (accessed March 30, 2007).

25. Michael Frost and Alan Hirsch, *The Shaping of Things to Come: Innovation and Mission for the 21st-Century Church* (Peabody, MA: Hendrickson, 2003), x.

26. Wheatley, *Leadership and the New Science*, 83–84.

27. Ibid., 83.

28. Ibid., 166–67.

29. Ibid., 99–100.

30. Cheyenne Urban Forestry Operation, City of Cheyenne Parks and Recreation Department, http://www.cheyennetrees.com/mission.html (accessed March 31, 2007).

31. Wheatley, *Leadership and the New Science*, 86.

32. Ibid., 66.

33. Ibid., 100.

34. Ibid., 104.

35. Gil Rendle and Alice Mann, *Holy Conversations: Strategic Planning as a Spiritual Practice for Congregations* (Herndon, VA: Alban, 2003), 56.

36. Wheatley, *Leadership and the New Science*, 98.

37. Ibid., 101.

38. William M. Easum, *Sacred Cows Make Gourmet Burgers: Ministry Anytime Anywhere by Anyone* (Nashville: Abingdon, 1995), 50.

39. Ibid., 52.

40. Wheatley, *Leadership and the New Science*, 108.

41. Ibid., 106.

42. Ibid., 107.


Chapter 2  *Complexity: An End to Childish Ways*

1. Carol Rausch Albright, *Growing in the Image of God*, Saint Paul University Research Series: Faith and Science, ed. Ivan Timonin (Toronto: Novalis, 2002), 24.

2. Ibid., 20.

3. Ibid., 21–22.

4. Ibid.

5. Ibid., 23

6. Ibid.

7. Ibid., 23–24.

8. Ibid., 24.

9. Ibid.

10. Paul Davies, "The Unreasonable Effectiveness of Science," *Evidence of Purpose: Scientists Discover the Creator*, ed. John Marks Templeton (New York: Continuum, 1994), 119; cited in Albright, *Growing in the Image of God*, 25.

11. Albright, *Growing in the Image of God*, 26.

12. Ibid.

13. Ibid., 27.

14. Ibid., 28.

15. Ibid., 38; italics in original.

16. For more on this subject, see William O. Avery, "A Lutheran Examines Fowler," in Jeff Astley and Leslie J. Francis, eds., *Christian Perspectives on Faith Development: A Reader* (Grand Rapids: Eerdmans, 1992), 122–34.

17. Steve Doughty, *To Walk in Integrity: Spiritual Leadership in Times of Crisis* (Nashville: Upper Room, 2004), 20.

18. Margaret J. Wheatley, *Finding Our Way: Leadership for an Uncertain Time* (San Francisco: Berrett-Koehler, 2005), 32.

19. Ibid., 75–84.

20. Ibid., 33.

21. Ibid., 89.

22. Wheatley, *Finding Our Way*, 36–41, points out that identity, information, and relationships are the three conditions of self-organizing organizations.

23. Ibid., 39–40.

24. Ibid., 40.

25. Ibid.

26. Cited in Michael Frost and Alan Hirsch, *The Shaping of Things to Come: Innovation and Mission for the 21st-Century Church* (Peabody, MA: Hendrickson, 2003), 7.

27. Margaret Wheatley, telephone interview, May 10, 2006.

28. Ibid.

29. Diarmuid O'Murchu, *Quantum Theology: Spiritual Implications of the New Physics* (New York: Crossroad, 1997), 129.

30. Ronald A. Heifitz, *Leadership Without Easy Answers* (Cambridge, MA: Belknap, 1994).

31. Wheatley, *Finding Our Way*, 30.

32. Ibid., 79.

33. Arlin Rothauge, *Sizing Up a Congregation for New Member Ministry* (New York: Seabury, for The Education and Ministry Office of the Episcopal Church, undated [1983]).

34. One of the best updates of Rothauge's work and the book that Bill uses in seminary classroom teaching is Beth Ann Gaede, ed., *Size Transitions in Congregations* (Herndon, VA: Alban, 2001), especially chapter 1, "Current Thinking on Size Transitions" by Theodore W. Johnson.

35. Alice Mann, *The In-Between Church: Navigating Size Transitions in Congregations* (Herndon, VA: Alban, 1998), 5.

36. See, as an excellent example of approaching children's "sermons," A. Roger Gobbel and Philip Huber, *Creative Designs with Children at Worship* (Atlanta: John Knox, 1981).

37. These stages are discussed in William O. Avery, "Enhancing Supervision Using Fowler's Developmental Theory," in Astley and Francis, eds., *Christian Perspectives on Faith Development*, 384–96.

38. Avery, "A Lutheran Examines Fowler."

39. James and Evelyn Whitehead, "On Assignment from God," audiotape. (Avery listened to this audiotape more than twelve years ago but no longer has the tape or knows where he obtained it.)

40. Martin Luther, "The Large Catechism," in *The Book of Concord*, ed. Robert Kolb and Timothy Wengert (Minneapolis: Fortress, 2000), 386.

41. For more on the whole matter of the steward, see John Reumann, *Stewardship and the Economy of God* (Grand Rapids: Eerdmans), 1992.

## Chapter 3  *Interrelatedness: Reconciling the World*

1. Diarmuid O'Murchu, *Quantum Theology: Spiritual Implications of the New Physics* (New York: Crossroad, 1997), 74; cited in Cletus Wessels, *The Holy Web: Church and the New Universe Story* (Maryknoll, NY: Orbis, 2000), 55.

2. Brian Swimme, *The Hidden Heart of the Cosmos: Humanity and the New Story* (Maryknoll, NY: Orbis, 1996), 34; cited in Wessels, *The Holy Web*, 55.

3. Carol Rausch Albright, *Growing in the Image of God*, Saint Paul University Research Series: Faith and Science, ed. Ivan Timonin (Toronto: Novalis, 2002), 23.

4. Bob Sitze, *Your Brain Goes to Church: Neuroscience and Congregational Life* (Herndon, VA: Alban, 2005), 5–6; Albright, *Growing in the Image of God*, 29.

5. Sitze, *Your Brain Goes to Church*, 7.

6. Albright, *Growing in the Image of God*, 14.

7. Stuart Grassian, "Psychopathological Effects of Solitary Confinement," *American Journal of Psychiatry Online* 140 (1983): 1450–54, http://ajp.psychiatryonline.org/cgi/reprint/140/11/1450 (accessed April 27, 2007).

8. Elaine Siemsen, "Ta Panta! All Things Restored!" *The Lutheran*, April 2004, 22.

9. "About Lutheran Services in America," Lutheran Services in America, http://www.lutheranservices.org/AboutLSA.asp (accessed April 28, 2007).

10. Margaret J. Wheatley, *Leadership and the New Science: Discovering Order in a Chaotic World*, 2nd ed. (San Francisco: Berrett-Koehler, 1999), 144.

11. Margaret Wheatley, telephone interview, May 10, 2006.

12. Daniel Goleman, *Working with Emotional Intelligence* (New York: Bantam, 1998), 299; Goleman's emphasis.

13. Margaret Wheatley, telephone interview, May 10, 2006.

14. Ibid.

15. William C. Placher, ed., *Callings: Twenty Centuries of Christian Wisdom on Vocation* (Grand Rapids: Eerdmans, 2005), 206.

16. William E. Diehl, *Ministry in Daily Life: A Practical Guide for Congregations* (Herndon, VA: Alban, 1996), 13.

17. See Gustav Wingren, *Luther on Vocation*, trans. Carl C. Rasmussen (Evansville, IN: Ballast, 1999), 245ff.

18. Ibid., 137.

19. Ibid., 172.

20. Douglas J. Schuurman, *Vocation: Discerning Our Callings in Life* (Grand Rapids: Eerdmans, 2004), 51, 157.

21. Ibid., 36.

22. Ibid., 60.

23. Frederick Buechner, *Wishful Thinking: A Seeker's ABC* (San Francisco: HarperSanFrancisco, 1993), 119.

24. Schuurman, *Vocation*, 135.

25. Ibid., 145.

26. Ibid., 146.

27. Ibid., 95

28. Ibid., 149–50.

29. Joan Chittister, "It's Time to 'Hunt the Words,'" *National Catholic Reporter Conversation Café* 4, no. 38 (March 29, 2007), http://ncrcafe.org (accessed March 29, 2007).

30. Elizabeth A. Johnson, *Women, Earth, and Creator Spirit: Madeleva Lecture in Spirituality* (New York: Paulist, 1993), 39; cited in Wessels, *The Holy Web*, 56.

## Chapter 4  *Diversity: For All of Us Are One*

1. Dan Geer, Rebecca Bace, Peter Gutmann, Perry Metzger, Charles P. Pfleeger, John S. Quarterman, and Bruse Schneier, "Cyber*In*security: The Cost of Monopoly—How the Dominance of Microsoft's Products Poses a Risk to Security," September 24, 2003, http://cryptome.org/cyberinsecurity. htm (accessed April 26, 2007), 2.

2. Ibid., 12.

3. Ibid., 10.

4. See Jamais Cascio, "The Ecology of Computer Viruses," *Salon.com*, April 7, 1999, http://www.salon.com/tech/feature/1999/04/07/melissa/print. html (accessed April 26, 2007), 1–3.

5. This phrase occurs in Juanita Brown, David Isaacs, World Café Community, and Margaret J. Wheatley, *The World Café: Shaping Our Futures through Conversations That Matter* (San Francisco: Berrett-Koehler, 2005), 103.

6. Jacques Derrida, *The Gift of Death*, trans. David Wills (Chicago: University of Chicago, 1995), 41, as quoted in Michael Jinkins, *The Church Faces Death: Ecclesiology in a Post-Modern Context*, Religion and Postmodernism Series (New York: Oxford University Press, 1999), 15.

7. For a much fuller treatment of this subject, see Jinkins, "The Church Faces Death: Ecclesiology in Search of Identity and Responsibility," in *The Church Faces Death*, 8–32.

8. Marcus G. Singer and Robert R. Ammerman, *Introductory Readings in Philosophy* (Dubuque, IA: William C. Brown, 1960), as quoted in Jinkins, *The Church Faces Death*, 100–101.

9. The thoughts in this paragraph were in part stimulated by a telephone conversation with Margaret Wheatley on May 10, 2006.

10. C. Peter Wagner, *Your Church Can Grow* (San Jose, CA: Resource Publications, 2001).

11. This sentence was voiced by Connie Kleingartner, professor at the Lutheran School of Theology in Chicago, in a conversation with the authors on May 3, 2006.

12. Nancy J. Ramsey, "Metaphors for Ministry: Normative Images for Pastoral Practice," *Quarterly Review* 17 (Spring 1997): 39–54.

13. Ibid., 40.

14. Ibid., 41.

15. Ibid., 42.

16. Ibid., 43.

17. Ibid.

18. Ibid., 45.

19. Ibid., 47.

20. Ibid., 48.

21. Beverly Wildung Harrison, *Making the Connections: Essays in Feminist Social Ethics*, ed. Carol S. Robb (Boston: Beacon, 1985), 12; as quoted in Ramsey, "Metaphors for Ministry," 49.

22. Ramsey, "Metaphors for Ministry," 50.

23. Ibid., 51.

24. Ibid., 53.

25. Ibid.

26. Ibid., 43–45.

27. Brown et al., *The World Café*, 204.

28. Among the many books coauthored by a scientist and a theologian, we mention one very recent book: Ted Peters and Martinez Hewlett, *Evolution from Creation to New Creation: Conflict, Conversation, and Convergence* (Nashville: Abingdon, 2003).

29. David R. Ray, *The Big Small Church Book* (Cleveland: Pilgrim, 1992).

30. Margaret Wheatley, telephone interview, May 10, 2006.

31. This statement was made by Connie Kleingartner in a conversation with the authors on May 3, 2006.

32. See Dennis Olson, "Moses, Manna, and Leadership," in Princeton Theological Seminary, Institute for Youth Ministry, *Cloud of Witnesses: An Audio Journal on Youth, Church, and Culture*, vol. 9, *Leadership*, http://www.ptsem.edu/iym/cow/vol9/index.php (accessed April 26, 2007).

33. The World Café Community can be contacted at inquiry@theworld-cafe.com or by calling 415-383-0129. Several of the following insights are from the book by Brown et al., *The World Café*.

34. Margaret J. Wheatley, "We Can Be Wise Only Together," in *The World Café*, ix; italics in original.

35. Ibid.

36. See Brown et al., *The World Café*, 101–2, 125–26, 134, 168, for a fuller description of this technique.

37. Ibid., 97.

38. Ibid.

39. Ibid.

40. Ibid., 99.

41. Ibid., 100.

42. Margaret Wheatley, telephone interview, May 10, 2006.

43. David L. Cooperrider and Diana Whitney, "A Positive Revolution in Change: Appreciative Inquiry," as quoted in "Intro to AI: What Is Appreciative Inquiry?" *Appreciative Inquiry Commons*, http://appreciativeinquiry.case.edu/intro/whatisai.cfm (accessed April 26, 2007).

44. Ibid.

45. Ibid.

46. The words "destructive diatribe" and "constructive dialogue" are used in an epilogue by Anne W. Dosher, "How Can We Talk It Through?" in *The World Café*, 214.

47. Brown et al., *The World Café*, 169.

48. Dosher "How Can We Talk It Through?" 214.

49. Ibid., 213.

50. Joseph R. Myers, *The Search to Belong: Rethinking Intimacy, Community, and Small Groups* (Grand Rapids: Zondervan, 2003).

51. For a discussion of the sister-congregation arrangement, see Gilson A. C. Waldkoenig and William O. Avery, "Milwaukee Strategy, Wisconsin," in *Cooperating Congregations: Portraits of Mission Strategies* (Herndon, VA: Alban, 1999), 111–45.

52. This conversation with Douglas John Hall occurred on October 31, 2005. The author did not have a tape recording of the conversation, so this comment represents a memory of what was said.

53. Jinkins, *The Church Faces Death*, 74.

54. Mark Noll, "American Lutherans Yesterday and Today," in *Lutherans Today: American Identity in the 21st Century*, ed. Richard Cimino (Grand Rapids: Eerdmans. 2003), 20, as quoted in Richard H. Bliese and Craig Van Gelder, eds., *The Evangelizing Church: A Lutheran Contribution* (Minneapolis: Augsburg Fortress, 2005), 1.

55. Jinkins, *The Church Faces Death*, chap. 1, esp. 28–32.

56. Ibid., 28.

57. Ibid. The treatment of Mead is found on pp. 58–63.

58. Ibid., 59.

59. Ibid.

60. Ibid., 60.

61. Ibid., 62.

## Chapter 5 *Process: An Invitation to Adventure*

1. Alfred North Whitehead, *Science and the Modern World* (New York: Macmillan, 1925; New York: Mentor, 1948), 70.

2. Edwin H. Friedman, *Generation to Generation: Family Process in Church and Synagogue* (New York: Guilford, 1985).

3. Ed. L. Miller and Stanley J. Grenz, *Fortress Introduction to Contemporary Theologies* (Minneapolis: Augsburg Fortress, 1998), 91. See also Robert B. Mellert, *What Is Process Theology?* (New York: Paulist, 1975), 11–12.

4. Frank Thilly, rev. by Ledger Wood, *A History of Philosophy* (New York: Holt, 1952), 307, as quoted in Carol Rausch Albright, *Growing in the Image of God*, Saint Paul University Research Series: Faith and Science, ed. Ivan Timonin (Toronto: Novalis, 2002), 35.

5. Albright, *Growing in the Image of God*, 36.

6. Mellert, *What Is Process Theology?* 13.

7. Ibid., 13–14.

8. William L. Reese, "Whitehead," in *Dictionary of Philosophy and Religion* (Atlantic Highlands, NJ: Humanities, 1980), 622, as quoted in Miller and Grenz, *Fortress Introduction to Contemporary Theologies*, 92.

9. Alfred North Whitehead, *Adventures of Ideas* (New York: Mentor, 1955), 43, as quoted in Miller and Grenz, *Fortress Introduction to Contemporary Theologies*, 92.

10. Miller and Grenz, *Fortress Introduction to Contemporary Theologies*, 92. See also, Edwin H. Friedman, *Family Process and Process Theology* (Herndon, VA: Alban, 2007), DVD.

11. Mellert, *What Is Process Theology?* 14.

12. Ibid., 15.

13. Marjorie Hewitt Suchocki, *God, Christ, Church: A Practical Guide to Process Theology* (New York: Crossroad, 1982), 10.

14. Friedman, *Family Process and Process Theology*, video.

15. Ibid.

16. Bernard J. Lee, *The Becoming of the Church: A Process Theology of the Structures of Christian Experience* (New York: Paulist, 1974), 3–4.

17. Clark M. Williamson and Ronald J. Allen, *Adventures of the Spirit: A Guide to Worship from the Perspective of Process Theology* (New York: University Press of America, 1997), 1.

18. Whitehead, *Science and the Modern World* (1925), 172, as quoted in Williamson and Allen, *Adventures of the Spirit*, 3.

19. Ted Peters and Martinez Hewlett, *Evolution from Creation to New Creation: Conflict, Conversation, and Convergence* (Nashville: Abingdon, 2003), 199.

20. See, e.g., Sjoerd L. Bonting, *Creation and Double Chaos: Science and Theology in Discussion*, Theology and the Sciences Series (Minneapolis: Fortress, 2005), 90, 144; and Miller and Grenz, *Fortress Introduction to Contemporary Theologies*, 100–102.

21. In fact, Peters identifies and locates on a scale many of the theologians who hold what he calls a position of theistic evolution. See Peters and Hewlett, "Chaos Theology: An Alternative Creation Theology," in *Evolution from Creation to New Creation*, 115–57, for a brief description of these theologians.

22. Peters and Hewlett, "Chaos Theory and Chaos Events," in *Evolution from Creation to New Creation*, 158–81, esp. 160.

23. Miller and Grenz, *Fortress Introduction to Contemporary Theologies*, 91.

24. Edwin H. Friedman, "DVD Study Guide," *Family Process and Process Theology* (Herndon, VA: Alban, 1990), 5.

25. Friedman, *Generation to Generation*, 2–3.

26. Ibid., 15.

27. Ibid., 19–39.

28. Friedman, *Family Process and Process Theology*, video.

29. Friedman, "A Study Guide," 10.

30. Friedman, *Generation to Generation*, 27.

31. Ibid., 27–28.

32. Friedman, "A Study Guide," 11.

33. Friedman, *Generation to Generation*, 35.

34. Friedman makes the comment about being 70 percent self-differentiated several times in his video.

35. Margaret J. Wheatley, *Leadership and the New Science: Discovering Order in a Chaotic World*, 2nd ed. (San Francisco: Berrett-Koehler, 1999), 153–54.

36. See J. Paul Balas, "Spirituality, Spiritual Formation, and Preparation for Pastoral Ministry," in Kirsi Stjerna and Brooks Schramm, eds., *Spirituality: Toward a 21st-Century Lutheran Understanding* (Minneapolis: Lutheran University Press, 2004), 13–14.

37. John Ackerman, *Listening to God: Spiritual Formation in Congregations* (Herndon, VA: Alban, 2001), 1.

38. Doug Pagitt and the Solomon's Porch Community, *Church Re-Imagined: The Spiritual Formation of People in Communities of Faith* (Grand Rapids: Zondervan, 2005), 19.

39. Balas, "Spirituality, Spiritual Formation, and Preparation for Pastoral Ministry," 23.

40. William O. Avery, "Field Education: Rich Soil for Seminarians' Spiritual Formation," in Stjerna and Schramm, eds., *Spirituality*, 127–28.

41. Balas, "Spirituality, Spiritual Formation, and Preparation for Pastoral Ministry," 28.

42. David Schimke, "Turn Up the Quiet," *Utne Reader*, July-August 2005, 54, as cited in Diana Butler Bass, *Christianity for the Rest of Us* (San Francisco: Harper, 2006), 120.

43. Bass, *Christianity for the Rest of Us*, 120.

44. Thomas Merton, *Thoughts in Solitude* (New York: Farrar, Strauss and Giroux, 1999), 50, as quoted in Bass, *Christianity for the Rest of Us*, 121.

45. Wheatley, *Leadership and the New Science*, 153–54.

46. Ibid., 155.

47. Pagitt, *Church Re-Imagined*, 21.

48. Whitehead, *Science and the Modern World* (1925), 168, as cited in Lee, *The Becoming of the Church*, 14.

## Chapter 6 *The Center: Where Trust Prevails*

1. Margaret J. Wheatley, *Leadership and the New Science: Discovering Order in a Chaotic World*, 2nd ed. (San Francisco: Berrett-Koehler, 1999), 34.

2. Peter B. Vaill, *Managing as a Performing Art: New Ideas for a World of Chaotic Change* (San Francisco: Jossey-Bass, 1989).

3. Bruce Mehlman and Larry Irving, "Treat Coming Data Flood as an Opportunity," *Minneapolis St. Paul StarTribune*, May 29, 2007, Wisconsin ed., sec. A.

4. Thomas L. Friedman, *The World Is Flat: A Brief History of the Twenty-first Century*, expanded ed. (New York: Farrar, Straus, and Giroux, 2005), 8.

5. Loren B. Mead, "Foreword," in Diana Butler Bass, *The Practicing Congregation* (Herndon, VA: Alban, 2004), x.

6. Ibid.

7. Loren B. Mead, "Foreword," in William O. Avery, *Revitalizing Congregations: Refocusing and Healing through Transitions* (Herndon, VA: Alban, 2002), ix.

8. Robert Banks and Bernice M. Ledbetter, *Reviewing Leadership: A Christian Evaluation of Current Approaches* (Grand Rapids: Baker, 2004), 53.

9. James M. Kouzes and Barry Z. Posner, ed., *Christian Reflections on the Leadership Challenge* (San Francisco: Jossey-Bass, 2004), 119.

10. Wheatley, *Leadership and the New Science*, 165.

11. Mead, "Foreword," in Avery, *Revitalizing Congregations*, x.

12. Gil Rendle and Alice Mann, *Holy Conversations: Strategic Planning as a Spiritual Practice for Congregations* (Herndon, VA: Alban, 2003), 103; emphasis is Rendle and Mann's.

13. Ibid., 104.

14. Ibid., 105.

15. Ibid.; emphasis is Rendle and Mann's.

16. Ibid., 109; emphasis is Rendle and Mann's.

17. Ibid., 110.

18. Margaret Wheatley, telephone interview, May 10, 2006.

19. Edwin H. Friedman, *Generation to Generation: Family Process in Church and Synagogue* (New York: Guilford, 1985), 22; emphasis is Friedman's.

20. Built on the foundation of work by Craig Dykstra, Dorothy Bass, and others, Diana Butler Bass has described this phenomenon most fully in three books: Diana Butler Bass, *The Practicing Congregation* (Alban, 2004); Diana Butler Bass and Joseph Stewart-Sicking, eds., *From Nomads to Pilgrims* (Alban, 2006); Diana Butler Bass, *Christianity for the Rest of Us* (HarperCollins, 2006).

21. Bass, *The Practicing Congregation*, 4.

22. Ibid., 14.

23. Ibid., 15.

24. Paul Hoffman, "Forming Faith: The WAY," in Diana Butler Bass and Joseph Stewart-Sicking, eds., *From Nomads to Pilgrims: Stories from Practicing Congregations* (Herndon, VA: Alban, 2006), 57–66.

25. Joseph Stewart-Sicking, "Christian Practices in the Congregation," in Bass and Stewart-Sicking, eds., *From Nomads to Pilgrims*, 4.

26. Ibid., 3.

27. Beth Ann Gaede, ed., *When a Congregation Is Betrayed: Responding to Clergy Misconduct* (Herndon, VA: Alban, 2006), xiv.

28. Ibid., xviii.

29. Ibid., xix–xx.

30. Deborah Pope-Lance, "Afterpastors: Restoring Pastoral Trust," in Gaede, ed., *When a Congregation Is Betrayed*, 57.

31. Robert K. Greenleaf, *The Servant as Leader* (Indianapolis: Robert K. Greenleaf Center for Servant-Leadership, 1970), 7, cited in *On Becoming a Servant-Leader*, Don M. Frick and Larry C. Spears, ed. (San Francisco: Jossey-Bass, 1996), 1–2; emphasis Greenleaf's.

32. Henri J. M. Nouwen, *In the Name of Jesus: Reflections on Christian Leadership* (New York: Crossroad, 1989), 63.

33. Greenleaf, "The Individual as Leader," in Greenleaf, *On Becoming a Servant-Leader*, 336; Greenleaf's emphasis.

34. "Patchwork Quilt," The Church of St. Philip, http://www.churchofstphilip.org/patchworkquilt.php (accessed May 25, 2007).

35. "Women of Great Hope and Vision," The Church of St. Philip, http://www.churchofstphilip.org/women.php (accessed May 25, 2007).

36. "The Patchwork Quilt Digital Divide Initiative Joins World Community Grid," The Church of St. Philip, http://www.churchofstphilip.org/pqstories.html (accessed June 8, 2007).

37. World Community Grid, http://www.worldcommunitygrid.org/ (accessed June 8, 2007).

38. "Patchwork Quilt Digital Divide" (accessed June 8, 2007).